P9-CEJ-062

LIFE IS NOT AN ACCIDENT

LIFE IS NOT
AN ACCIDENT

A MEMOIR OF REINVENTION

•

JAY WILLIAMS

HARPER

An Imprint of HarperCollins*Publishers*

LIFE IS NOT AN ACCIDENT. Copyright © 2016 by Jay Williams. All rights reserved. Printed in the United States of America. No part of this book may be used or reproduced in any manner whatsoever without written permission except in the case of brief quotations embodied in critical articles and reviews. For information, address HarperCollins Publishers, 195 Broadway, New York, NY 10007.

Excerpt from *A Return to Love* by Marianne Williamson © 1992 by Marianne Williamson. Used with permission from HarperCollins Publishers.

HarperCollins books may be purchased for educational, business, or sales promotional use. For information, please e-mail the Special Markets Department at SPsales@harpercollins.com.

FIRST EDITION

Designed by Renato Stanisic

Library of Congress Cataloging-in-Publication Data has been applied for.

ISBN: 978-0-06-232798-7

16 17 18 19 20   OV/RRD   10 9 8 7 6 5 4 3 2 1

This book is dedicated to my extraordinary parents, David and Althea Williams, who have been by my side every step of the way to help me become the man I am today.

Our deepest fear is not that we are inadequate. Our deepest fear is that we are powerful beyond measure. It is our light, not our darkness that most frightens us. We ask ourselves, "Who am I to be brilliant, gorgeous, talented, fabulous?" Actually, who are you *not* to be? You are a child of God. Your playing small does not serve the world. There is nothing enlightened about shrinking so that other people won't feel insecure around you. We are all meant to shine, as children do. We were born to make manifest the glory of God that is within us. It's not just in some of us; it's in everyone. And as we let our own light shine, we unconsciously give other people permission to do the same. As we are liberated from our own fear, our presence automatically liberates others.

—Marianne Williamson, from *A Return to Love*

CONTENTS

•

LIFE IS NOT AN ACCIDENT

1

Perfect

•

On the day I almost died, I remember waking from an afternoon nap to the full glory of the sun hanging over the lake like the tip of a sparkler. The master bedroom in my place in Chicago had floor-to-ceiling windows and a wraparound deck with a patio that connected to the living room. You could turn left and see the skyscrapers. Turn to the right and there was Lake Michigan, looking as limitless as an ocean. It was one of three modern-inspired units on the 40th floor of the Park Hyatt on Michigan Avenue. I had been there just about a year, and every time I opened the front door, I would step into the foyer in shock at how my life had drastically changed. It was spectacular.

In places like Los Angeles or Miami, you take days like June 19, 2003, for granted. But in Chicago, where the winters are so cold, dark, and long that the locals call it Chiberia, days like these are treated like precious jewels. While standing in front of the window in my bedroom, I took a deep breath and gazed upon my new city of dreams. I reached out and pressed my hand against the window to feel the warmth of the light and thought to myself, *Today is going to be an amazing day.*

One of my dreams growing up was to have multiple homes. It just seemed like one of those things that symbolized real success. So during my rookie year with the Chicago Bulls, I rented a home in Deerfield near the team's practice facility, in addition to this sleek 2,300-square-foot luxury condo in the heart of downtown Chicago. Since my parents wouldn't let me touch my actual NBA salary, both places were covered by the money I had already made from endorsement deals. Looking back, this was one of the times when their control over me turned out to be for the best.

So many people look at what happened to me later that afternoon through the prism of a ruined NBA career, but that's not how I think about it today, or at least that's not the only way I think about it. The way I see it, it's a reminder of how things can change in a flash. There's a saying that a sense of immortality is a curse carried only by the young, but I disagree. We all do it—take the future for granted. That's just human nature. Then one day you wake up in your perfect apartment on a perfect day, with your perfect job, leave for a meeting, and never see that perfect apartment again.

The day before, I had flown down to Durham, North Carolina, to talk to some students at a basketball camp at my alma mater, Duke. Afterwards, I played pickup ball with some of the Duke players while Chris Collins, who was still an assistant under Coach Mike Krzyzewski at the time, watched. This was my first time playing against J.J. Redick, who was one of the greatest players ever to play at Duke. J.J. and I were on separate teams in a pickup game, and I loved how as a freshman his ego was almost as big as mine. Almost. He was fiery and competitive and reminded me very much of myself. I picked one of my best friends, Graham, who had just finished a solid career at Appalachian State, to be on my team—but J.J. insisted on enforcing the unspoken rule that only Duke players have the right to play in the first game. J.J. was already on his way to taking Christian Laettner's throne as the most disliked Duke player. I remember looking at him and saying, "Are you fucking kidding me? I picked Graham and he is going to play on my team. That's final." What had already slipped my mind, not even a year removed from playing college ball, was that at Duke, rules are rules. It was not only embarrassing to get overruled by a freshman leading the way, but even more so that it happened to be in front of 600 campers. Whether right or wrong, I felt disrespected on a court where I had accomplished way more than anyone there at the time. So I walked Graham over to the sideline and told him, "Enjoy the show." I was angry, and I knew what was coming.

The game went to eleven baskets and I scored nine, all on J.J.

I had just finished my rookie season as a pro, and it was the most up-and-down year I'd ever had—on and off the court. Our journey wrapped in April, since we didn't make the postseason—we were 24 games out of playoff contention—and I immediately headed to the gym to work my ass off for the following season. I was determined to come back with a vengeance.

I hadn't realized how much I had improved, but Chris Collins saw it right away. "Man, you've been working on your game, huh? Your game has gone to another level," he said. "You are going to dominate the league next year if you keep playing like that."

The next morning, I got up to take a crack-of-dawn flight home to Chicago. When I got to my condo downtown, I threw my bags down, got undressed, and fell right into bed to take the first of two power naps that day. I wouldn't have bothered setting my alarm if I hadn't already committed to a workout at the Berto Center as well as a meeting with my marketing agent, Kevin Bradbury. Kevin had set up a brainstorming session for us with a tech guy about my new website later that afternoon. When the alarm went off, I forced myself out of bed. I always found an aux-iliary source of energy when it came to basketball. With Coach Collins's comment that I was going to dominate the league ring-ing in my ears, I was excited to head straight to the gym.

The Berto Center was the Bulls' practice facility then. The place was a pantheon for many of the legendary memories from the Jordan era. There, for about five years, the most famous player in the world wielded his trade in the hangar-like complex, ex-changing elbows and trash talk with the likes of Scottie Pippen, Steve Kerr, and Dennis Rodman. The walls were covered with all kinds of championship banners—divisional, conference, world—which served as a reminder of how far off the deep end the fran-chise had plummeted.

The workout that morning was with some of my teammates. As usual, Jamal Crawford and I went at it. Only this time, some-thing felt different . . . in a good way. My legs weren't heavy like they'd been the entire year—the adjustment from playing 40 games in a college season to 82 as a pro had been gruesome. I left the workout thinking this was going to be my year. It was all starting to click.

I was running on fumes as I made the hour-long trip back to my place downtown. I finally got home, tossed the keys to the truck on the counter, stripped down, and crashed.

•

As I woke up to that beautiful summer afternoon, I was even more drained than before. Within the past 24 hours, I'd been in Durham playing ball, partied that night into the wee hours of the morning, caught the first flight back to O'Hare, a nap, a training session, another nap—and here we are.

As much as I wanted to bail on the meeting Kevin had set up, my dad had raised me to keep my appointments; so I dragged myself out of bed, again, and started to get ready.

My closet looked like an Adidas Foot Locker commercial. I had a multi-million-dollar deal with them, which entitled me to an unlimited allotment of apparel each year. I felt like the man, getting paid to wear their stuff, and I laugh about it today when I see what guys like Derrick Rose and James Harden get paid for endorsements. The crazy thing is that I never got the chance to wear most of the clothes because of what would take place later that day.

I threw on one of my countless white Adidas T-shirts, my favorite blue jeans, and a pair of Adidas classic shell-toe sneakers. I was running behind. My dad wouldn't approve.

I had a deal with Chevrolet at the time. They gave me a Tahoe and a Corvette as part of the agreement. The SUV was perfect for the Chicago winters, but it wasn't winter. It was summer. *Finally.* And a perfect day at that. The Corvette always made me feel like a 55-year-old man trying to recapture his youth, so I decided to take my motorcycle out instead. It was a black Yamaha R6 with red accents.

There's a lot to adjust to when you first come into pro ball. No one is on you to make sure you get to classes—there are no classes. There isn't anyone monitoring you to see if you're putting in your time at the gym or in the weight room. Your time is your own to manage. I thought I was ready for it, but like any other naive 21-year-old, I had no clue.

At Duke, we were like a family. Coach K insisted on it, but the older players were the ones who really watched over us when we were underclassmen. We didn't want to let those guys down. We pulled together, looked out for one another, and stuck to the script. There was only one agenda, and it was a collective one: Do things the right way, and win.

Things couldn't have been more different that year with the Bulls. When the average age of your team is 23, a new guy coming in didn't represent help. It meant somebody's job was in jeopardy. We were in competition—for minutes, for shots, for stats, all of which would translate into money down the line. I wasn't used to looking around the locker room and wondering if there was anybody I could trust. And I sure as hell wasn't used to losing. In my first five weeks in the pros, we lost as many games as I had during my three years at Duke. It was mind-boggling to see guys play like they didn't care, and it really took its toll.

Basketball had been my one outlet, the place where I could take whatever frustration, anger, or sadness I was feeling and transfer it into the physical and mental rush of competition. It was on the court that I had always found solace, and now, for the first time in my life, I was turned off from the game. And I had no backup plan when the one thing I relied on to blow off steam became the cause of all my problems.

But I did have money. And time. And soon, I had a motorcycle.

I can't remember exactly how my obsession with bikes began. I had seen photos of Michael Jordan riding all kinds of exotic motorcycles as a player and remember thinking how badass he looked. I wanted to look a certain part, I wanted to be my own man, and I wanted to rebel. For some inane reason, I was convinced that riding a bike would check all those boxes.

I would be lying if I said no one warned me about motorcycles. They did. But the more everyone told me I shouldn't be riding a bike, the more I wanted to ride. We all know how that works.

I had worked my ass off to become an NCAA champion, a two-time national player of the year, and the second pick of the draft, and yet I had this team of people around me always telling me what I should or shouldn't be doing. Especially my parents, who seemed to have an opinion about every last decision that involved me. I wanted—no, I needed—to make my own decisions, to have some control over my own life. The Yamaha R6 symbolized that for me.

But I was that prototypical young hotshot who thought he had all the answers. For starters, I had never taken a single riding class. Motorcycle license? What for? Money and arrogance were all I needed. I walked into the first and only bike shop I'd ever been in, saw the R6, and bought it on the spot. And that was that.

If you've ever ridden a motorcycle, you know the instant adrenaline rush it provides. The wind is blowing in your face, and you can feel each and every mile per hour you're going. I never appreciated how moving even 40 miles an hour felt until I got a motorcycle. You can hear all of the street fragments kicking up as you drive over them, your legs straddling the engine as if you're attached to a human-size rocket. It gave me a heightened sense of awareness and power, reminiscent of the rush I got on the court. The good *and* bad news ended up being that I wasn't afraid of it at all.

I started hanging around bike shops, buying gear. Eventually I met a group of guys who liked riding at high speeds late at night, when there were fewer cars on the road. I should've been nervous, but I wasn't. In the spring of 2003, I would meet up with this crew and ride down Lake Shore Drive, or sometimes take I–90 over to Indiana, passing cars at 130 miles per hour. I know it sounds crazy, but I'd never felt so powerful in my life.

I was looking for what I'd lost when I left college: camaraderie. So we rode. Guys on my left would be standing vertical on the seats of their bikes while they were going 30 miles per hour. Other guys on my right were laid out like flying angels while revving their engines to decibel levels that were out of this world. I had never seen anything like it before. I tried a trick or two, but it was mostly just the speed that I was after.

It was the most eclectic bunch of guys I've ever been with. Lawyers, teachers, mechanics, black, white, Latino, Native American, some covered in tattoos, others squeaky clean. It was this incredible cross section of humanity, but we all had one thing in common: we loved to ride. And that's what we talked about—not our day jobs, personal lives, or anything else except the rides we'd taken or the ones we planned to take.

I KEPT RIDING with them until one night, one guy I barely knew lost control of his bike and crashed. He was ahead of me on the right of the "peek" going about 90 miles an hour. His front wheel started to wobble and he lost control. It was the scariest thing I had ever seen. The bike flipped, and his body flew for what seemed like forever. When he finally landed, he hit the highway like a rock being skipped across a pond. All of us stopped immediately to barricade the accident area from other vehicles. As I approached him, there was blood everywhere and his body looked torn apart. We all surrounded him and waited for the ambulance to arrive. He ended up only suffering a few broken bones, but it was enough to scare me from ever riding at those speeds again, though not enough to give it up entirely. I couldn't; it meant too much to me.

THE MEETING WITH Kevin and the tech guy was only a couple of miles away, so I instinctively grabbed the keys to the bike. I didn't bother grabbing my helmet, since it was a gorgeous day out and I wanted to feel the sun on my face. To be honest, I hardly ever wore a helmet—it wasn't against the law in the state of Illinois— but I did put on a jacket, which I left open so it could flap in the wind. The garage in the building was actually aboveground, and I loved pulling out of my spot and cruising down the spiral entry- way to ground level. I would always rev the engine a few times while in neutral on the way down. There was something I loved about hearing the sound of the exhaust echoing off the walls. It was obnoxiously loud and would always grab people's attention. Apparently being the new face of the city's NBA franchise wasn't enough for me.

The meeting went great. I was really happy with the progress we were making with the website and was excited to see the finished product. I gave Kevin a hug and told him how much I appreciated him. He was more than my agent; he was a big brother to me. We'd first met when I was 17 years old and he was working for a marketing firm that handled the McDonald's All American Game and surrounding events. He ended up chaperon- ing me in New York City for a *Rosie O'Donnell Show* appearance. He was one of the few people I trusted enough to talk to about all the issues with our team during that time. Kevin would always remind me to keep my head up and stay encouraged, and that all my hard work was going to pay off.

At the end of our meeting, Kevin asked me what else I had planned for the day, and I told him, "I have no clue. Just headed home and maybe another workout." We walked out the front door of the home where the meeting had taken place and I climbed on my bike as we continued talking about this and that.

"You shouldn't be riding that thing," he said.

"Kevin, I shouldn't be doing a lot of things," I said.

A few minutes later, I was bleeding to death.

THERE WEREN'T A lot of people around when I was driving away, but I revved my engine anyway. Kevin was still standing in the doorway watching, and I wanted to make sure that he heard my new exhaust. As I coasted down the street, I revved the bike twice—the second time louder than the first. Then, in the middle of my third rev, I heard a *click-click* sound and the bike popped up and shot off. My first thought was that the gears had slipped and I had to control the situation. If I had just let go of the motorcycle, chances are I would've walked away with some bumps and bruises. Maybe a broken arm. But I held on.

My hands were already on the handlebars; the front tire was in the air, and I was almost trying to wrestle it to the ground. My grip tightened as I tried to hold on, and maybe that even revved the throttle a little more. I must've accelerated by 20 miles an hour in a split second as the back wheel aggressively spun out of control, abruptly redirecting me to the right while forcing me to lean backwards, which was the last thing I wanted to do. I was terrified that I was going to slip off the back and have the bike fall directly on top of me. Looking back, that would've been a way better scenario. But I leaned forward, looking down, trying to use all my weight to get the front wheel back down . . .

And then I saw it . . . the pole.

It was too late. All I could do was tense up, prepare for the impact, and hope for the best. I distinctly remember that in the split second between recognizing I was about to hit the pole and making contact, I actually thought, *This* should *happen to me.* During that year, I had constantly lied to the people I cared about. I had cheated left and right on the woman I loved. I had become infatuated with the money, the lifestyle, and the constant attention that came with being an NBA player. It took less than a year to become someone I didn't recognize, and I thought in that fraction of a second that I didn't deserve an outcome different from the one that was coming.

I couldn't tell you which pole I hit, but the crash sounded like two cars colliding head-on. I couldn't turn my body completely out of the way, so I ended up clipping my entire left side, which flung me into a horizontal spinning motion parallel to the ground. In those seconds, everything seemed to slow down. While in the air, I remember thinking, *You've seen this before. You lived this before.*

And I had, incredibly, in a dream four years prior, a dream so strange it had stayed with me. . . .

It was the night before the first game I ever played for Duke—in Madison Square Garden, no less, at the Coaches vs. Cancer Classic—and I was trying to sleep in my bedroom at the

Marriott Marquis high above Times Square. In the hotel, my teammates and I were separated from the rest of the world: it was our safe haven, where we could focus on the mission at hand.

But I was too anxious to fall asleep. I was about to play Stanford in *the Garden*, the place I had dreamed of playing at since I was a little boy growing up in Plainfield, New Jersey, just 25 miles away. I was heading into my first game starting for a Hall of Fame coach who had just lost the national championship to UConn only seven months prior, in a game his team was expected to win. I was about to play the biggest game of my life in the shadows of all the Duke greats. Guys like Grant Hill, Christian Laettner, Bobby Hurley, Johnny Dawkins. *And* I'd be playing before the nation, on ESPN.

Finally, after hours and hours of tossing and turning, I dozed off. Soon I felt this magnificent, incredible breeze on my face. But I was getting dizzy. In the distance up ahead I saw something that I was going to crash into . . . and then I jerked awake. It was four fifteen in the morning. I sat up in my bed, thinking, *What the hell was that?!*

Was that, somehow, a sign, a warning, and I missed it?

Looking back, I've wondered if the fact that my Corvette keys were in front of my Yamaha keys that morning was also a sign I ignored. I definitely ignored the countless warnings about the dangers of motorcycles from people who cared about me. The last thing I heard before getting on my bike was Kevin, my mentor, telling me not to ride—and I hadn't listened to him or anyone. I was in control. I was making my own decisions. I was being a man.

And now here I was, flying in the air and spinning. In control of nothing.

The impact when I landed was immediate, like an anchor being dropped into water. I was facedown. My chest was lying directly flat on the grassy area between the curb and the sidewalk; my legs lay outstretched on top of each other, almost disconnected from my body on the pavement at a 90-degree angle. My lower extremities were motionless as the curb pressed against my abdomen.

I began screaming Kevin's name over and over again. I was in so much pain and unable to move, from my midsection down. I was certain that I was paralyzed. With my cheek flush against the grass, I could see Kevin running toward me. As he got closer, I remember his mouth opening wide in shock, almost in disbelief at what he was seeing. All the color left his face as he stood over me, horrified. It looked as if someone had reached into his body and yanked out his soul. His expression was all the confirmation I needed about what I had done. I started crying and pounding my right fist against the grass while yelling, "I threw it all away! I threw it all away! I threw it all away!"

Kevin yelled for help while pulling out his cell phone to dial 911. I started to feel the sensation of someone pouring a pitcher of scalding hot water from my pelvic area down to my feet. I went into shock as the pain began to override my senses. Kevin was holding my hand, telling me everything was going to be all right, but there was nothing believable about his tone. Everything was not going to be all right—ever again.

I was inconsolable as I ricocheted from anger to sorrow and back to anger and then sorrow once more. It felt as if time had stood still. I hoped I was having another dream, just like the first one, and soon I would wake up. How could this be real?

I had done this to myself. And the pain from that reality, as I would soon discover, would not be tempered by morphine, and would last long after my broken bones had healed. As I lay there on the ground, the lower half of my body now feeling like it was on a bed of burning embers, I couldn't help but think that seeing that biker break his collarbone during one of my late-night rides was yet another sign I had ignored.

"It's going to be okay, you're going to be fine," Kevin repeated, desperate to get me to calm down.

I was slowly bleeding to death internally.

I wasn't even sure I wanted to live.

Not long before, I had been lying in bed, gazing out my window at the turquoise waters of Lake Michigan as sunlight tickled the waves. I had a business meeting with one of my best friends in the world. I was going to hit the gym and maybe grab some lunch afterwards. Today was going to be amazing. Today was going to be perfect.

2

Imperfect

•

B y the time the ambulance arrived, I had calmed down slightly,
enough to try and answer the paramedics' questions.

Do you know your name?

Yes . . . I am Jay Williams!

Do you know what just happened to you?

Yes, yes, yes . . . I just hit the damn pole and I can't feel my fucking legs.

So you don't feel me touching your legs?

I knew the medic had good intentions, but I was in so much
pain that I quickly started to lose my patience with his simple
questioning. There was only one question on my mind.

Am I paralyzed?

He thought for a second and then told me that I would be just
fine. As they continued to assess me, one of them said, "I think
you've just broken a couple of bones."

Having been the daredevil that I was as a kid, I knew what

it felt like to break bones. This was something different. Broken bones would've been a gift. This was a pain that had exceeded any other pain I had ever felt. I wouldn't have wished this on my worst enemy . . . and now it was my reality.

Were they just minimizing the severity of my injuries to try and keep me calm? Was I hearing what I wanted to hear instead of the cold, hard truth?

Deep down I knew that I would never be the same.

As they tried to gently adjust my body to lay me directly on my back, it felt as if my insides were being ripped apart. The pain was so excruciating that I begged them to stop.

"Stop. Stop. Stop. Get the fuck off me. Please. Get off me. Just let me be."

They delicately placed my neck in one of those mobile braces to keep me from causing any further damage. Once I was stable, ever so slightly, they tilted my body just enough to slip a board under me. I was then lifted onto a gurney and rolled into the ambulance. As the adrenaline kicked in, the pain took a backseat to fear. I was wailing so much that it felt impossible to catch my breath.

Just before they put me in the back of the cabin, I yelled to Kevin, begging him to let me use his cell. I dialed the only phone number that mattered. As the phone rang, my heart was pounding through my chest. *Pick up, pick up, pick up.* As desperate as I was for someone to answer the phone, I knew what would happen the minute I heard my mom's voice. I wouldn't have been able to keep myself together. My dad probably would have tried to keep his cool for my benefit, but hearing my mother's voice would have broken me.

I got their machine. Not knowing what to say, I tried my best to sound calm. "Hey, Mom and Dad, it's me. I've been in a really bad accident. I think I'll be okay, but you guys need to come to Chicago as soon as possible. I love you both so much. Please get here." Not the message a child wants to leave behind for his parents, but it's a lot better than hearing the same news from a stranger. At least this way I had a chance to get to them before the news broke.

The ride to the ER was a complete blur. An IV into my arm, oxygen mask over my face, and a ton of chatter as they assessed my vitals, with Kevin by my side the whole time.

The next thing I remember, I was being gurneyed into the ER at a frantic pace while a woman was sprinting by my side to let me know that I was at Illinois Masonic. "Jay, my name is Dr. Mellett. You've severed a major artery in your left leg. We have to stop the bleeding *now*." Panic began to set in once again with a lot more urgency.

"I don't want to die. I don't want to die."

And no one was telling me that I wouldn't.

As I lay on the cold, sterile operating table, broken, halogen lighting beaming down, Dr. Mellett stood by my side, firmly clutching my hand. I had no idea where Kevin was, or anyone I knew, for that matter. I was alone, surrounded by complete strangers in scrubs, accompanied by a doctor who, just moments ago, was one of them. Now she was my crutch, her voice my only source of comfort. The only thing I was moving was my eyes, scanning my surroundings in terror. My one friend in the room then spoke.

"Jay, look at me. Just focus on me. Focus on your breathing. In through your nose, out through your mouth. Just take one breath at a time. It's going to be okay."

As the anesthesia began to take, I thought about my parents.

Would I ever be able to see them again? I had so many things I wanted to tell them. For starters, how sorry I was for not listening to them. Sorry for trying to prove my manhood by doing something so foolish. Sorry for not being a better son. Sorry for everything.

In what could've been the last few seconds of my life, I was thinking about everything I had just thrown away. I tried to keep my eyes open, afraid to go under. My eyes would shut and then jolt open, trying to fight the effects of the anesthetic to the very end. I didn't want to let go. What if I didn't wake up?

As I slowly opened my eyes, not knowing if hours or days had passed, my blurred vision started to give way and I began taking in all my surroundings. My eyes first took account of all the metal rods and bars that were holding my broken body together.

This can't be real.

I then realized I had a tube jammed down my throat and I immediately felt like I was suffocating. I saw Kevin by my bedside. He looked exhausted. His face was pale, his eyes bloodshot as if he had been crying for days. It was hard for me to look him in the eye. I was ashamed. Completely emasculated.

What had I done? This was not just my future, but Kevin's, too. And my parents? Where were they? *I've ruined everything for them.* My dad had always wanted to have his own business. I made that dream possible and, in the most selfish fashion, took it all away. My eyes teared up; the emotions were too much.

Kevin took my hand. He was at a loss for words. It then occurred to me that he must've felt like a failure at that very moment. My parents had trusted him to look after me, and the accident happened on his watch. Even now, I can't imagine the amount of guilt he had, even though the truth is that nobody would've been able to stop me from this path of self-destruction. Both of our futures were now crushed.

I was completely covered in bandages from the waist down and my left leg hovered in the air, held up by three metal rods inserted deep into the bone for stabilization. Two more rods, one on each side, were placed into my hips to keep the pelvic bone from further separation. Those rods extended out of my body by a foot or more, at 45-degree angles, all connected by wires.

My initial reaction was to move my feet. Nothing. I tried to move my legs. Nothing. *Nothing fucking worked.*

I mustered up enough strength to lift my right arm and point to my mouth. I wanted Kevin to tell the doctor to remove the tube from my throat. He left the room to get someone to help. I was alone for the first time. A dangerous place to be. Those five or so minutes lying there by myself was the beginning of a tortured hell that would haunt me for the next decade of my life. I was trapped in my own head, having to keep myself from drowning in self-pity.

Yes, I was alive, but what did that mean? Was I paralyzed from the waist down? Did I want to be alive if I couldn't play—or even walk—anymore? The answer was NO. I wished I had died earlier that day rather than live with this cursed sentence. I wasn't grateful at all to be alive. After years and years of questioning myself on the court, I had just started to realize that I was able to do things other people couldn't. I had been a deeply insecure child through adolescence, and playing ball gave me the confidence I needed for my everyday life. What did I have left if I didn't have basketball?

I was alive—and it was killing me.

The doctor entered to remove the tube from my throat. The

process felt like a hot cord was being pulled up from the bottom of my stomach through my esophagus. Once the discomfort subsided, I tried to speak, but to no avail. The doctor told me to just remain calm, that it was completely normal and that he'd be right back with my primary doctor—my friend, Dr. Michele Mellett, the woman who had saved my life.

When she walked into the room, it seemed as if time had stopped. I wish today that I had thanked her on the spot for saving my life. And for being that one soothing voice that helped to keep me in one piece. But I didn't—because at that time, I was selfish.

I tried to talk but could only muster a soft whisper. She leaned in as I once again asked her the only question that was on my mind.

"Will I ever be able to play again?"

There was a pause as I watched her eyes scan my body and then meet my eyes, taking inventory of my state of mind before answering. I guess that was the smart thing to do, considering I had just been in a life-threatening accident and the first words out of my mouth were about basketball. Not "Where am I?" or "Where are my parents?" or maybe "Thank you for saving my life." I asked her the only question that could provide me with some immediate relief. If she answered yes, I'd know that everything would eventually be okay. But if she said no, it would mean my life would be—well, I didn't even want to think about it.

The look on her face said, *How do I tell this guy I have no clue?* She was expressionless. And the silence was deafening. After what felt like an eternity she said, "Let's not focus on playing basketball. Let's just focus on trying to get you to walk again." And then she stood, holding my hand, not knowing what to say next.

My mind flashed to a game against Stanford in Anaheim during my sophomore year at Duke. We were down a couple of points, and I dribbled the ball the full length of the court in just five seconds to shoot a layup. I missed the shot, but that wasn't the point. I was lightning quick on my feet, and I had only gotten faster. Now . . . I had to focus on just being able to walk? Yesterday I was beating Allen Iverson off the dribble and now I had to start all over? And she hadn't even said it with much conviction, but more as an open-ended statement. Like even walking might not be a possibility.

I didn't want to be here anymore. It was like someone had put a five-ton weight on my chest and I couldn't breathe. I've always been a guy who wanted to prove pundits wrong. News articles ripping me, fans yelling at me, or even those closest to me not thinking I was good enough—I relished the criticism. This was the first time in my life I felt truly defeated. Completely powerless.

"I'm not going to be able to walk," I whispered to myself. I looked over to Kevin for strength, or even a glimmer of hope. But the moment was too heavy even for my big brother to carry. We both just sat there staring at each other in silence, lacking the energy even to pretend I might be wrong.

Within the next hour or so, my parents arrived. I had never seen my dad cry. I'd heard his voice get shaky on the phone once, but he'd never let me see any tears. As they walked into the room, his eyes grew heavy with pain and sorrow. I know how disappointed he must've been with me for putting my life in jeopardy. I deserved to get a serious talking to from him. But in that moment, he was just my dad. He grabbed my hand, kissed me on the forehead, and began to weep silently. I knew he loved me more than anything, but he was from a generation that didn't always express emotion. I guess nothing can prepare you for seeing your child's body in that state. Seeing his face, my mom's face, Kevin's . . .

It was all too much.

I know each person standing around my bed was happy I was alive. Of course they were—they were my family. But being alive felt more like a consolation prize than anything else. Watching their facial expressions that day confirmed what I already knew deep down. The chances of me playing basketball again were slim. That likely meant all of our long-term plans were shot to hell. My mom had worked multiple jobs, gone back to school and become an education administrator. She began to work on projects with Arne Duncan, who was in charge of Chicago's public schools at the time; he would eventually become Obama's secretary of education and almost assuredly would've taken my mother to greater heights she could've only dreamed of.

I had embarrassed Duke, Coach K, the Bulls franchise, and all of the Bulls' fans. When I got drafted, I wanted to change the game—not just on the court, but off it, too. I was going to take full advantage of my college education by leveraging the economic opportunities that came with being an NBA player. I had graduated school in just three years. The platform the NBA was going to provide was limitless with the right business plan attached. I was determined not to be a dumb jock, but I became the dumbest of them all.

Going out after hours trying to create the persona of J-Will, the Renegade Biker, flying like Icarus way too high for my own good, I was lucky not to get caught by the police—or, worse, have my brains splattered all over I–90. I was fearless, heedless, too arrogant to appreciate the gifts God had given me. I flew closer and closer to the sun until the inevitable happened—crash and burn.

At this point the mental anguish was far more intense than the physical agony I was in. The only relief was morphine, and that would prove to be the beginning of a long and troubling road of self-medicating.

It's common for patients in the ICU to lose the ability to track time, due to irregular sleeping hours and heavy medication. Sometimes I would wake up at two in the morning with a jolt of pain in my pelvis and be up until that evening. Nurses constantly checked in to make sure they knew the number of my pain on a scale from one to ten. The answer was always the same. *Fifteen.*

Pumped full of painkillers and suffering from sleep deprivation, I began to hallucinate. A week or so into my stay, I told my dad I was going crazy. Every time I closed my eyes, I would hit the pole. Over and over again, each time harder than the last, while hearing that horrible cracking sound of the bike colliding with the pole. Another night, I woke up and started screaming for help because I thought my bed was on the ceiling. My dad grabbed my hand and told me that he was right next to me, and I would yell, "Help me. Please help me. You're not next to me, Dad. I am on the ceiling, you are on the ground, and I am trying to reach you. I can't reach you. Why won't you help me?" It was scary losing control of not only my body but my mind as well.

It wasn't until a week or so later that Kevin decided to share with me just how bad my injuries were. He told me how the doctors had been unsure if they'd be able to save my left leg. Or whether I would survive the surgery to stop the internal bleeding.

I still don't know how many surgeries I had after the accident. My left knee was totally dislocated, every ligament torn. I'd completely ripped my hamstring off the bone. My pelvis was dislocated. I'd severed the peroneal nerve in my left leg. There is a scar that runs from my ankle all the way up to my mid-thigh on the outside of that same leg, courtesy of the fasciectomy the doctors performed in order to save my leg. I also split a major artery, causing displaced blood to begin to fill the leg. To relieve the pressure, surgeons made a series of deep incisions in my leg, essentially filleting it, to release the blood. I needed more than 100 staples to patch the muscle and skin back together. Afterwards, I couldn't bear to look at my body; it was unrecognizable, and the pain still lingers on today, though not as intense.

Just four days later, while I was still in the ICU, the NBA draft took place, and the Bulls selected Kirk Hinrich from Kansas with the seventh pick overall. All it took was one visit, days earlier, from our newly hired general manager, John Paxson, to make up his mind. He replaced me. There's a reason why Paxson is still the executive VP of operations for the franchise. Like he had in his playing days, he ended up with a clutch pick as Hinrich turned into a solid pro.

I WAS IN bed, unable to recognize myself as I drifted in and out of consciousness, just staring at the tiles of a popcorn ceiling above. The drugs helped only so much to block out the moans and screams coming from patients in other rooms. The smell. An odor that exists only in a space where many are crying and bleeding, clinging to life. The morphine drips couldn't trickle down fast enough. I would open my eyes, take one look at what I'd done to myself the night before, and pass out again. This was my second night in ICU hell at Illinois Masonic.

The next day—don't ask me what time—a figure emerged from the doorway of my room, walking toward me. At first I just assumed it was a doctor or someone else who worked there. But all it took was a couple of steps and I knew exactly who it was.

Three years earlier, around the time I committed to Duke, Coach K had undergone joint replacement surgery for his left hip. Ever since, his gait would favor one side over the other. It was a walk I knew all too well. We locked eyes, as we had so many times before; tears streamed down both of my cheeks as he clutched my right hand. I was overwhelmed with emotion—my second father had arrived. I blacked out once again.

I was groggy when I came to, which was when I looked to my right at K, still holding my hand.

"I'm never going to play again." I began to sob.

I had been mourning all that I had thrown away, and now I was overcome with guilt, ashamed that I had let him down.

He let go of his firm grasp, reached into his pocket, and took out a pendant. He told me it was his mother's rosary as he put it in my hand.

"Give this back to me when you play again, because you are going to play again."

I looked directly at him, but that wasn't good enough for him. He demanded that I *hear* him and *feel* what he was saying.

"Look at me," he said with conviction. "You're going to play again."

I am certain he was distraught seeing one of his many sons in such a horrifying condition, but he refused to show sadness or disappointment. Instead he stood by my side, not allowing me the option of giving up.

Of all the memories I have of playing for Coach K—and I have many—that moment in Illinois Masonic is my fondest. He will always give every ounce of himself to help you become the best version of yourself. It doesn't stop when you're done playing for him. If you need him, he's there without your having to ask.

That's a man. That's a coach.

AFTER CLOSE TO a month at Illinois Masonic, Coach K and Duke went out of pocket to fly me in a private medical plane to Durham, where I was admitted to Duke University Hospital for another month. In August, my parents rented a house in Durham, where I spent countless days in a hospital bed that was brought in.

It was the first time in about six and a half weeks that I was sleeping in a house and not a hospital. I was high on OxyContin and virtually out of it on a regular basis. The drugs numbed the physical pain but didn't do anything to quell the mental agony I was in. They plunged me into my own personal hell. I had nothing but time to think about the accident and what I had done to myself.

I became obsessive about how I was going to handle confronting the world. This was before the social media era, when something like this would've been impossible to escape from. Rather than tweets and postings, I received literally thousands of handwritten letters from people all across the world. The story had gone global.

WILLIAMS' CAREER IN JEOPARDY AFTER MOTORCYCLE CRASH

BULLS' GUARD JAY WILLIAMS BREAKS LEG IN MOTORCYCLE ACCIDENT

JAY WILLIAMS'S FUTURE CLOUDY AFTER CRASH

I fantasized about the things people were saying to one another at work, at the gym, while out for dinner. Everywhere. Things like *I wonder if he's ever going to be able to walk again . . . What a fucking moron . . . There goes the money.* All the things I could imagine myself saying if the shoe were on the other foot.

In my darkest moments, I would think about never being able to have sex again. The pelvis injury had caused such severe nerve damage that I'm lucky to be able to get an erection today. I would wonder if I would even be able to have a family one day when the time was right. And if so, would I ever be able to show my kid how to round first base or shoot a layup? It was a compilation of one depressing thought after another, leaving me on the edge of a cliff, readying myself to jump.

One evening, my mom left the room and I noticed on my nightstand a pair of scissors that was used to change my bandages. Without a second thought, I stretched as far as possible to grab them. Being able to reach them was an accomplishment in its own right, considering I could barely move. The fact that I had them in my hand seemed like a sign that I was meant to kill myself. It was as if they had been strategically placed there by some divine power letting me know what I should do.

With my right hand, I opened the scissors and held one of the blades against my left wrist. When I looked at the tattoo on my wrist—BELIEVE—I hesitated for a couple of seconds, and then drew the blade directly across the word, thinking, *I don't believe in shit anymore.* I was so physically weak, and the blade so dull, that no matter how many times I tried, I couldn't cut deep enough. The Oxy probably didn't help my coordination, either. I was so frail and emaciated—my arms were the size of sticks, and I weighed 140 pounds, 55 less than on the day of my accident—that after each superficial cut I was physically drained.

On my third attempt to open a vein, my mother walked into the room, saw what I was doing, and in a frantic state grabbed the scissors out of my hand.

"Jason, are you trying to hurt yourself?!"

"Mom, I don't want to be here anymore. I don't think I can live with what I've done to myself."

She started crying hysterically, begging me to promise I would never try to take my life again. Then she grabbed my hand and started to pray.

I guess God was not done with me yet.

3

Gray Area

•

When I was growing up in Plainfield, New Jersey, my parents threw these fantastic parties at our house. I loved having people over, because that meant laughter and good company. Being an only child had its obvious advantages—no annoying siblings and a room to myself—but it also got lonely at times. Maybe that's why I overthink things so much as an adult, never having had brothers or sisters to talk to while growing up. At these get-togethers, there were plenty of kids my own age to hang out with, and I got to see my parents behave very lovingly toward each other. In some ways they may have been putting on an act for guests, but I'd like to think that maybe it helped rekindle something genuine between them.

My mom, Althea Bowman Williams, is outgoing, energetic, the kind of person who comes to life when people are around. She's also incredibly well-spoken and intelligent. After college she became a teacher, but my earliest memories were of her working as a guidance counselor. When I was in elementary school, she decided to go back to college to earn additional degrees in education. Not long after I left home for school, she accepted a position as principal at Plainfield High School.

My dad, David Williams is more reserved than my mom, preferring to spend quality time by himself either reading, working, or playing with the dog. It's not that he's antisocial; he was just always more comfortable at home, his safe haven where things are the way he likes them to be.

They met and fell in love at "the" Ohio State University—as they have trained me to say since birth. But when my dad accepted a job in Manhattan with American Express, my mom instead decided to move to California to live with her aunt. He stayed in constant touch and eventually convinced her to move back east so they could be together. As romantic as that sounds, their relationship became defined by a constant push and pull.

We lived in a lower-middle-class neighborhood in Plainfield— but literally right down the street from what most people would consider a bad area. Gangs, drugs, and fights at Cedar Brook Park, where I used to go to shoot hoops, were the norm. And I was too young at the time to know any different. All I cared about was minding my own business and finding a basket for myself. I would stay there for hours playing imaginary one-on-one games. My mom and dad had no problem with me going there.

It was a totally different story when it came to my education. My parents wanted to insulate me from the bad influences that were all too common in the local public schools. So from preschool on, they sent me to private schools. First it was Montessori, followed by Sacred Heart, and then St. Joseph's to round things out.

I remember when I was really young, fourth grade or so, there was an announcement over the school PA that they would be holding basketball tryouts. I'd been working on my game—all I could do at that point was shoot the ball with two hands from beside my right ear—and I was so excited that I ran home from the bus stop, threw open the screen door, and started yelling, "Mom! Mom! There's a shoot-out! There's a shoot-out!" She immediately grabbed me and pulled me to the ground, saying, "Get down! Get down!" She wanted to shield me from any stray bullets. When I realized what she was doing, I said, "No, Mom—basketball shoot-outs!" The word had a whole different meaning at the school she worked at, a place where you had to pass through a metal detector when entering the building.

My dad came from a big family in Fort Lauderdale, Florida. His mother, Elizabeth Snelling Williams, was a prominent civic activist and leader in the community, working on causes ranging from at-risk youth to proper care for the elderly. She always prioritized education; in the 1940s, she campaigned for African American students to have a full school term each year, rather than having it cut short so the students could go work the harvest. The city of Fort Lauderdale named a street after her—Elizabeth S. Williams Boulevard. In 1984, she was honored at the White House as matriarch of a Great American Family, for putting all ten of her children through college.

My dad loved sports, and he passed that love on to me. He had his own way of watching a game. He'd be upstairs in his room and you'd hear this loud stomping sound—*Boom! Boom!*—as he pounded his foot on the floor. Or *Boom! Boom! "No! What the hell are you doing?!"* as he yelled at the screen in frustration. But then out of nowhere we'd hear him laugh; it was the most infectious laugh in the world. The most random things would crack him up—if a commercial struck him as funny, out came this burst of laughter that always put a smile on your face.

Because he loved tennis—and was a big fan of Ivan Lendl—I learned how to play the game at a very young age. I also played soccer before I ever took up basketball, because there was a strong Latin influence in the town and that was the sport of choice. By second grade I was playing both of those sports, and I am convinced they helped a great deal once I started basketball, thanks to the footwork from soccer and the hand-eye coordination from tennis.

Once I was watching a Pete Sampras match with my dad. This was when he was dating the actress Kimberly Williams. They would show her in the stands, and my dad would start telling me how women can mess up your game, how you have to dedicate yourself to your sport if you want to stay focused, and how they have the power to distract you if you let them. I shrugged it off then, but looking back, I have to admit there was one loss in particular, at Florida State, that validated my dad's theory.

When my parents threw a party, my mom would cook these great dinners and you'd hear the soaring voices of Patti LaBelle, Aretha Franklin, James Brown, and others singing in the background. Everyone was always just so happy being together and kicking back. I was taught to call my parents' friends "aunt" and "uncle." Uncle Allen was my dad's best friend, and my mother later became friends with his wife, who was Aunt Diane. Uncle Tony and Aunt Chris were the parents of my close friend and "cousin" Jared. My dad's friends would arrive with a whole bunch of alcohol to go along with the feast. We were one big, racially mixed family having a blast.

When I was young, my parents would always try to get me to go to sleep by eleven P.M. on Christmas Eve, which was always a challenge, considering how loud things got downstairs as the evening went on.

One year my dad told me, "You better go upstairs, because Santa Claus is going to call you." And I'm like (insert Kevin Hart voice) "Oh my God! Oh my God! Santa is going to call me? Great, I'm going to tell him what I want for Christmas!" My dad told me to make a quick list of all the things I wanted. In our house there was one set of stairs near the living room and another by the kitchen. The kitchen stairs were still a little high for me, but in my excitement I took them, slipping and hitting my head on a step.

"I'm okay, I'm okay," I yelled. "I gotta go write to Santa."

So I have this huge knot on my head now, and I'm upstairs writing down this list when all of a sudden my dad yells from downstairs.

"Pick up the phone. Santa's calling!"

"Hello," I say.

"*Ho-ho-ho!* Is this Jason?"

"Yes, this is Jason . . . Is this Santa?"

"Yes, this is Santa. Now tell me what you want for Christmas."

The voice on the other end sounded like the most ghetto version of Santa possible. The way he asked what I wanted sounded like he was sticking me up. I could hear the laughter coming through the phone. I might've been young and naive, but I wasn't stupid.

"This isn't Santa. This is Uncle Allen."

"This isn't Uncle Allen. This is Santa! Now tell me, what do you want for Christmas?"

Meanwhile, I started to sneak my way down the front staircase.

I saw my Uncle Allen on the phone and my dad cracking up in the corner.

"You all trying to trick me," I said.

And my dad was just laughing and laughing. My father's laugh was one of the greatest gifts of all.

To understand how my mother fell in love with my dad, how he managed to convince her to move back from California, maybe even why she stayed with him as long as she did, all you have to do is hear him laugh. That isn't hard to do, because once he starts, you can hear him in every room in the house. Jared, my friend Dre, and I all tried to imitate it, because it's the kind of laugh that is infectious. He stomps his foot and loses his breath, with these short bursts of "Oh shit," "Ohhh, ohhh," "My God" in between. It was one of the most joyous sounds of my childhood.

But with two strong personalities like my father and my mother under one roof, there were bound to be some clashes. I heard them shouting and arguing more often than I like to remember. My mom can be scattered, like she has a little ADD in her; she'll start in on something and then get distracted and maybe come back to it or maybe not. My dad always wanted things to be where he left them; if he put a book or a tool someplace, he expected to find it there, even weeks or months later. My mom would clean up and put things where she thought they should go, sometimes forgetting where that was.

This triggered some nasty fights. I'd hear them yelling, and I wanted to hide and cover my ears. I wished I had a brother or sister, someone to provide perspective or comfort or just to share what I was feeling. That was especially true on those occasions when things got physical.

One day when I was in the fourth grade, my mother picked

me up from school, waiting for me in her maroon Mazda 929. I hopped in the car and saw that she was wearing these large, Jackie O–style shades. I could see that her lips and cheeks were swollen. I knew why. While I didn't witness my father hit my mother, I wasn't oblivious to the evidence he left behind.

Later that evening, my father came home accompanied by two police officers. I could see him at the back door, underneath the porch light. After repeated knocking and no answer, he yelled, "Open the damn door!"

I was trembling, because I didn't know what was going on or how to even react. My mother started yelling at him through the door, and continued to do so once he came in. The police officers escorted my father out once he had grabbed some of his belongings. The rest of that evening was awful as my mother cried the entire night while I did my best to console her.

Relatives and friends were aware of this occurrence, but no one called 911. No one thought about keeping her from going back home to him. My best guess was that she was thinking of me and not her own well-being. To this day, we as a family have never fully discussed my father's violent behavior. I'm their only child and I still don't know how to fully confront this part of my past.

My dad and I have spoken only once about his hitting my mom. It was during a therapy session after my accident. He was there; she wasn't. The therapist asked me, "Who are you, Jason? Who do you think you are as a person?" and I talked about being a combination of my parents. I told him I felt lost without basketball and that I was lucky to have my parents there to help me through this difficult time. Not everyone who had been in my life when I was riding high stuck around for this part of the trip.

I spoke to the therapist about the power struggle I had with my dad and how much I wanted to prove to him that I could be my own man. But with a broken body, being my own man was harder than ever. I was dependent on him—again. I told the therapist about a recent confrontation my parents had had where they were both up in each other's face. My dad had pushed my mom to get her out of his way. My first instinct was to step to him, which would have been a first; however, I was stuck in my fucking wheelchair. Go figure—the only time I ever conjured the courage to confront my dad out of respect for my mom was when I didn't have the ability to physically stand up. I just screamed and yelled at the both of them to please stop. I felt like that little kid back in fourth grade who didn't know what would become of his parents when emotions got out of control.

That session was a defining day in my life, because it was the first time I had ever heard my father express genuine remorse about the things he'd done, the decisions he'd made. He didn't go into specifics about particular incidents, but he said, "I . . . I made mistakes. I was a different person back then. I was working a lot, I was drinking a lot . . . and, well, I'm really sorry for it." He was extremely emotional, a side of my father I rarely saw.

Sitting at that table across from him, hands clenched tightly, I stared intensely into his eyes, listening to him talk filled me with a mixture of confusion and anger. I truly wanted to forgive my father, but I honestly didn't know if I had the capacity to do so. Truth be told, I had imagined this moment countless times before and knew exactly what I would say to him. I would say, *Your apology isn't good enough. Why would you do this to our family?* I would unleash years of pent-up frustrations and rage about how his actions made me feel. How they had changed the way I thought about him. I would tell him exactly how I had always felt.

But just as I was about to unload on him, my father made eye contact with me and said, "Jason . . . I am sorry about everything. I hurt you and I hurt your mother, and I will never forgive myself for that. I am not the man now that I was then. I am not perfect, but I promise to never hurt either one of you ever again."

I just sat there in my wheelchair at a complete loss for words. Actually hearing him say those things in that moment caused me to reflect on all the mistakes I had made in my life. I realized I needed to learn how to try and forgive people for their mistakes if I was ever going to learn how to forgive myself for mine.

The therapist locked eyes with me and said, "Forgiving someone isn't something that happens overnight, Jason, but your father's apology is a great place for that process to start."

It's an ongoing process for me. I still have moments of frustration when I see my mother's reaction to something that triggers those dark memories. But all I can do is continue to pray for her to never feel that pain again. I still don't know if my dad has ever sincerely apologized to my mom, or if he has, whether she ever fully forgave him.

My parents have lived apart for many years now. My dad still lives in the house I was raised in, while my mother is down in Durham, in a house that I bought when I was 21 years old. They've never gotten divorced, and they talk on the phone every day. I often wondered why my mom stayed with him through all the chaos. Maybe she felt it was what was best for me at the time. She told me on more than one occasion that she "signed up for marriage, not divorce." I think the whole situation is difficult, but it's their lives and I try not to judge. I just want them to be happy.

When I was at Duke, I heard a lot of writers and broadcasters go on about my family; Dick Vitale would be on ESPN extolling the virtues of my parents, this perfect college-educated black couple like the Huxtables. Duke was often criticized for bringing in only kids from that kind of family and avoiding the much larger population of athletes from broken homes or more modest backgrounds. Those critics usually mentioned Grant Hill and Shane Battier. And me.

I let them talk, knowing that the truth was more complicated than the narrative.

Sometimes when my parents fought, I just had to get out of the house, and do the one thing that was always my outlet.

Basketball.

Three times a week, my mother and I would drive down the Garden State Parkway to see my grandma in East Orange, whom I'd always called Grarock, a combination of "Grandma" and "Fraggle Rock" that was the best I could do as a small child. Every time we came to the tollbooth, my mother would have me shoot a quarter and a dime from the passenger seat into the toll basket. It became part of our road trip routine. One day, we pulled up to the booth and I missed a shot. The cars were lining up behind us, honking and cursing like typical Jersey people when there is a delay. My mother just calmly searched for another quarter and dime—for at least five minutes—and she then told me that we weren't going anywhere until I hit the basket.

By fourth grade, basketball had become my main focus. I had just gotten a brand-new ball, and like an idiot I left it outside in the rain one evening. The next day when I picked the ball up, it was pretty much flat. When I tried to dribble, the ball barely bounced to my mid-shin. But asking for another ball was out of the question, so I just made do with a flat one. I did all the drills I had learned from going to basketball camps, all the while bouncing this underinflated ball. I really had to pound it to get it to bounce back up where I wanted it, which helped me develop an even faster handle in the long run.

I was always playing against kids who were older than me. In fourth grade I made it through those "shoot-outs" and played junior varsity with all fifth- and sixth-graders. My coach, Mr. Morgan, was an older guy who wore Crocodile Dundee hats and rocked a white beard. He was a creative guy, so during one of the first weeks of practice he assigned everyone nicknames, wrote them down on tape, and stuck the tape on our lockers. Striker. Criminal. Cool, right? Of course, the nickname he gave me was Sweetness, which was clearly not as cool as the others. So I asked Coach Morgan, "Hey, Coach, why the name 'Sweetness'?"

"Because your game is sweet," he said.

I just stared at him with this look that said "Really?"

At the park, though, "sweet" wasn't going to cut it. I had brought my underinflated ball one day and got involved in an intense three-on-three game with a bunch of older kids. There was one kid in particular on the other team named Corey whom I didn't care for. He and his friends were about five years older than me, and they ran the court—the neighborhood, too. I had gotten jumped a couple of times by his crew, but that never stopped me from going to the courts to hoop.

During the game, he threw elbows to my face, sometimes even punches while going up for rebounds. He was physically so much stronger that there was nothing I could really do except take the abuse and play on. My team found a way to win the game, and afterwards everyone just started shooting around with my ball. When Corey grabbed the rebound, he looked at us and said, "I'm out of here," and he and his boys just took my ball and started walking away. I called after them, "Hey, that's my ball!" They just laughed and said, "If it's your ball, why don't you come and get it." And when I did, I most definitely "got it," all right. They jumped me again, knocking me down to the pavement while kicking me for added measure.

I got home, bruised and bleeding, and went straight up to my room to sulk. The next day, my dad asked me where my ball was and I told him I'd lost it. Naturally, he started questioning me about the last place I had it. He then suggested we go out looking for it, expressing the value of taking care of our things. I knew I couldn't keep up the lie, so I finally told him that some guys from the park had taken it from me. And I remember him saying, "What did I tell you about letting somebody take something that's yours? You don't let that happen. You go get your damn ball back."

I didn't know how I was going to do that. I went down to the park to scope out the situation; they weren't there that day, but the next day was Sunday, and sure enough, there they were, shooting around with my ball. I knew I needed to do something, to make it a little painful for them, but it had to be quick, in and out, before they knew what was coming.

I ran home and darted into the garage, where all I could find was this little kid-size wooden baseball bat. I went back to the park, biding my time until there was an opening. When Corey and the rest of his crew weren't looking, I snuck up on his weak side, took the bat, and hit him in the calf almost as hard as I could.

He went down, and I grabbed the ball and took off like Usain Bolt. A couple of the guys chased after me, but I had a good head start. I didn't want them to follow me to my house, so I tore into the woods, then circled back and made it home without anyone being the wiser.

My heart beating through my chest, I kept looking out my living room window, wondering if they had spotted me. Once I realized I was safe, I felt this surge of pride: *I got my damn ball back!* It was the first time I'd really taken ownership of something. *This ball is MINE.* I fought for something that meant a lot to me.

It set the tone for how I viewed basketball for a long time. I played my best when I was angry. If there was a loose ball, it was going to be *mine.* Even if the ref called a jump ball, I held on to it just to make sure you understood that the ball was mine.

I saw Corey several times after I pulled that Tonya Harding stunt. We definitely had a few more scuffles, but as I advanced as a player, I went to the park less often. And when I did return years later at around 16, I was already one of the top players in the area. The sport had begun to give me street credibility. Some of those same kids who had jumped me years earlier were now giving me serious respect, to the point where they were protective of me.

By sixth grade I was starting on the middle school varsity squad with seventh and eighth graders, even though I still had a two-handed, double-pump jump shot. I began playing on Amateur Athletic Union teams when I was 10 and found myself up against 13-year-olds, and at that age three years is a huge gap. Around eighth grade, I met a guy named Rich Leary, who coached an AAU team called the New Jersey Demons. I worked out with his team and got knocked around by better players, including future Villanova point guard John Celestand. The Lakers ended up drafting him with the 30th pick back in '99. Rich would pit us against each other every day, which was an uphill battle, to say the least. It was also exactly what I needed. I learned some valuable lessons from the experience: never taking a play off, not harping on mistakes, and refusing to back down.

I'll never forget when Rich brought us to play against Riverside Church at the famous Gauchos Gym in New York City. I was the youngest kid on our team and was in awe watching the other team warm up. They were 17-year-old kids with the bodies of 28-year-olds: Elton Brand, Lavor Postell, Erick Barkley, Ron Artest—or whatever he renamed himself recently. They were doing 360s, windmills, taking off from outside the paint, while we were barely able to slap the backboard in our layup line.

We got destroyed that day, but Rich played me the entire game. Turnover after turnover, Rich wouldn't let me quit, no matter how much I begged him to take me out. Each time-out he would pull me to the side and say, "This is a learning experience, Jason. Eyes . . . Eyes . . . You stay in the fight. You hear me? You don't quit." He always demanded eye contact when he spoke to us. As a broadcaster today, I can't help but notice how many players refuse to look their coaches in the eye when being spoken to, which I find infuriating.

That same year, my eighth-grade team went 42–0, since we were going up against kids our own age for once. We called ourselves the UN because of all our different ethnicities. Pete was white, Dre was Filipino, Brian was so black we nicknamed him Darkness. I saw color, but I didn't "see" race. As I said, my "aunts" and "uncles" came from all walks of life. And although Plainfield was mostly black and Hispanic, New York was just an hour's drive north, so I was constantly exposed to the melting pot.

As well-intentioned as my mother was, she couldn't keep me entirely out of trouble. I had my crew from home in Plainfield—the brothers Alvin, Brent, and Collins, whom I called ABC. Not brothers because they were black, although they were, but because they were actually each other's siblings. We used to find ourselves in a ton of mischievous situations, from egging houses late at night to throwing rocks and breaking windows, and even some graffiti. I wasn't necessarily the best sketch artist, but I would always leave my mark, which was a small slash through a *W*. I guess you could say I thought of myself as a young Picasso.

We would often sneak out and cut through my neighbors' backyard to get to the other side of the block, using a pathway between my neighbors' garage and ours. One summer day, ABC and I were ripping and running like usual. We were playing a game of manhunt and using both my backyard and that of the neighbor directly behind my house. He quickly became agitated and screamed at us for tearing up his lawn.

As a result, he and his neighbor decided to put up a massive wooden wall between their garages to cut off our access to the other side of the block. Truth is, I'd probably been annoying him for a long time before that day. When I played basketball in the backyard, I would throw the ball against the back of his garage as hard as possible to use as a pass for my next shot.

One day he climbed to the top of his new fence, pointed at me, and cursed me out. Afterwards, I decided to take matters into my own hands; my next "masterpiece" would be on his fence. I gathered some spray-paint cans and got to work. I knew he was a Pistons fan, so I decided to write, in big, capital letters, BULLS. (Chicago and Jordan dominated the Pistons at the time.) Then I spray-painted the chalk outline of a dead body on the ground with a sad face. And let's not leave out the little note I painted under it: BOOM YOU'RE DEAD. I also spray-painted my full last name instead of my personalized signature: ~~W~~.

I wanted him to know, without a doubt, whose work this was.

The only issue was, my dumb ass didn't spray-paint *his* side of the fence; I spray-painted mine. The next day, my father saw what I had done and took me to task. Not my proudest moment, and unfortunately my dad has the pleasure of seeing my artwork to this day.

The irony from the piece is too much for either of us to handle. I end up getting drafted by the Bulls and came millimeters away from becoming a chalk outline myself.

Boom you're dead.

IN PLAINFIELD, I struggled to fit in. I lived in between two very different worlds. At school, I was considered the athletic black kid. Classmates would say things like, "Jay you're so black, man. You're from the hood!" Meanwhile, after school I'd visit my mom at her job at Plainfield High School and get called out by the kids there for "acting white." Their reasoning was that I spoke articulately, was involved in student council, and wore a school uniform. They'd say, "You're such a little white boy," "You're so proper," "You're soft." I was very attuned to people's perceptions—and, in many cases, misperceptions—of me. I didn't know what more I had to do to prove myself.

This internal conflict continued through high school when I went to St. Joseph's, a Roman Catholic private school about nine miles away in Metuchen, instead of Plainfield High, which was only a block from my house. It was the mid-nineties, when hip-hop was blowing up and sagging your pants was the look. And there I was in a shirt and tie, going to a school where you would get detention if your shirt was untucked.

There was this constant shift between two entirely different cultures. During the day I would speak with correct grammar, and after hours I would be hanging on a street corner talking in slang. I was uncomfortable in my own skin. This preoccupation of having to transition from "acting white" to "acting black" every day was exhausting and a huge source of anxiety.

It was a big part of the reason I felt lonely in the NBA. I wanted to fit in. I wanted to be part of a family like I was at Duke. But we all know how black people all too often viewed players like me.

He's a sellout because he went to Duke. Duke recruits Uncle Toms—not real brothers.

After all this time, for this to *still* be an issue is absurd. Am I not supposed to educate myself? Should I choose to not be articulate? I remember trying to fit in by saying "nigga" a lot, and now I look back and wonder why I would ever use that term to refer to another black person, or anybody, for that matter.

My dad not only preached to me about what it meant to be a man, but he also showed me what hard work and dedication looked like. He woke up every morning and put on a suit, saying, "Dress for the job you want, not the job you have." My mom, the high school principal, was equally impressive in my eyes. The two of them showed me that hard work pays off and that it's not about where you came from or how you look.

For so long I struggled with my identity. If I'm blessed to have kids one day, I'll be damned if I ever let them feel as conflicted as

I was growing up. I will do my best to guide them on the important things in life. Not their ethnicity, religious identity, sexual
preference—those are just labels. All that matters is being a good
person and putting in the work.

Of course, issues of race still play a major role in my life today.
There are stigmas that come with being a black man. One example would be the women I choose to date. I'm obviously aware
of the stereotype of black men who date or marry white women,
and why it would upset many black women. But my love life is a
personal choice, not a political statement. I've dated black women,
I've dated Hispanic women, I've dated Asian women, and . . . I've
dated white women. I don't know what color of skin the woman
I marry is going to have. I *do* know that she will be kind, loving,
intelligent, and that I'll cherish her as much as possible.

I am not blind to racism. I've been pulled over by police for
no reason down in North Carolina more than once. In college,
I remember when a group of us decided to spend a weekend at a
friend's home in South Carolina. On the drive down, we stopped
at a bar in the sticks. We were underage but thought we'd try to
have a drink anyway. The place had an antique popcorn machine
and reeked of sour beer. I noticed the camouflage shirts on the
patrons as they stared me down, but I didn't think too much of it.
I was too busy rehearsing my order, fake ID in hand.

"We don't serve your kind here, boy," the bartender said.

I thought he was referring to the fact that I went to Duke or
that I wasn't of drinking age yet.

"Excuse me?" I said, with as deep a voice as I could muster.

"We don't serve niggers," he clarified.

I just stared at him in disbelief. After waiting a moment to see if it was a joke, I came to the conclusion that he was drop-dead serious. I turned around and we quickly exited the building. Thankfully unharmed.

Black does not mean ignorant. White does not mean "the correct way." I've had some people—people I still love to this day—say in front of their friends, "Come on, Jay, you know you aren't really black." Ignorance.

When I was in college, the public saw me through the lens of a story created by the media, one they thought they knew.

I guess we know now that things weren't so perfect around the Huxtables, either.

4

Rafters

•

had never been invited to the ABCD Camp until the summer heading into my senior year of high school. It was an All-American camp held at Fairleigh Dickinson University, in my home state of New Jersey. I always held a grudge against them for overlooking me, so, being the spiteful person I was then, I chose to accept an invite to the Nike All-American Basketball Camp, in Indianapolis, instead.

In high school, I played every position but point guard; go figure. That position belonged to Nick Cerulo. My high school coach, Mark Taylor, thought I was better off focusing my attention on scoring. I went to the Nike camp wondering how I would be able to differentiate myself from all these other top players. The thing was, *everybody* there could score. Some of those guys were averaging 35, 40 points a game in high school, and here I was, averaging a measly 24. I needed a plan.

I had only one or two guys on my high school team who were athletic. One guy in particular, 6'6" Paul Bocage, was our center. He also played volleyball and had an incredible vertical leap, but he had to be in certain spots for me to throw him the ball where I knew he could catch it. Now all of a sudden I'm surrounded by guys who are 6'8", 6'9", with 40-inch verticals, who are able to shoot threes and catch anything thrown their way. So I decided I was going to showcase my court vision and focus on making everyone else better. *Just go in, pass, and keep everybody involved*, I said to myself. And it worked.

In the first scrimmage, I had 17 assists and really started to find my groove. During the second scrimmage, I spotted Coach K on the sidelines. I also saw Roy Williams, who was at Kansas at the time. Kentucky's Tubby Smith, UConn's Jim Calhoun, Jim Boeheim out of Syracuse. The list went on and on.

But what really caught my eye were a couple of guys wearing North Carolina T-shirts. See, growing up, I wore my Tar Heel shorts—the heavy mesh Nike ones with a powder blue base and white accents—and I would lower the rim attempting to imitate the 360-degree dunks that UNC's Vince Carter did. Phil Ford was a legend, Kenny Smith was from Jamaica, Queens, and who didn't love watching Jerry Stackhouse play? I really didn't follow the ACC a lot, because I lived in Big East country. It was a gritty style of play where a fight threatened to break out every game. It reminded me of Cedar Brook Park, and I loved it. My dad was infatuated with coach John Thompson at Georgetown. Duke? I was aware of Bobby Hurley, whose father, Bobby Hurley Sr., coached the basketball powerhouse St. Anthony's in Jersey City. But nobody I knew was trying to be the next Bobby Hurley or his fellow Duke star Christian Laettner. It's funny, considering how things panned out, but in high school I really didn't pay attention to Duke at all.

I wanted to be a Tar Heel.

It was nerve-wracking playing in front of all these coaches. Every time somebody made a mistake, you would look over to the sideline and see these legends writing you up, like you'd committed a crime. When you did something good, it was the exact same response. They jotted down every small detail—the way you interacted with teammates, and your coach, how you dealt with the refs, with the opposing players, whether you used profanity, even if your shirt was tucked in or not. Most of all, we were being assessed on how we competed—did any of us slack off or, even worse, coast for stretches at a time?

One of the camp directors told me I averaged 16.5 assists per game. I didn't realize I had it in me. For the first time in my basketball career, I discovered how excited and happy people were to play with a guard who got them the ball in positions to succeed. It was rewarding for me making my teammates better.

All my life I've been told by others what I couldn't do. I would perk up whenever criticism came in my direction. Those slights—justified or not—have always stuck to my memory dartboard. When *Street & Smith's* basketball annual came out, I wanted to be on the list of the best players—no, I wanted to be at the top of the list. A year earlier, Coach Taylor had strongly suggested that I commit early to Fordham. I was ranked behind guys like Brett Nelson and Jason Gardner. Both were fantastic talents at the time, but being graded below them only inspired me to work harder, with more urgency.

Things escalated quickly coming out of the Nike camp. Letters from major programs started to flood my mailbox, and phone messages left by big-time coaches came by the dozens. I started to get recognized the way I had always dreamed about. It was incredibly validating. The hard work was beginning to pay off.

When it came time to make a decision about where I would go, my parents did a great job making sure there was a system in place for talking to coaches. My dad treated the process very much like a business. He would say, "Hey, you have Roy Williams calling at four thirty; Tubby Smith calling at four forty-five; Mike Krzyzewski at five o'clock; Dean Smith at five twenty . . ."

It was surreal.

A coach at a very prestigious university was on a conference call with us, and as usual, my dad was asking all the right questions. *What are most of your student-athletes majoring in? What is the political science program like? What kind of relationships do you have with your former players? Tell us about the alumni base. Can you recommend a list of players that we can speak with about their experiences?* The call was going really well. Every answer impressed us all. The school was shooting to the top of my list, and I couldn't believe it. Then, right before we hung up, my dad had one more question.

"What is your graduation rate, Coach?"

Pause.

"You know, David, I need to get back to you with that."

I watched my dad's face change from excitement to resignation. Down goes Kentucky!

I often wonder, if the man on the other end of the phone had been John Calipari, would my life have turned out differently?

I'd heard about some of the things that come with recruiting and campus visits. I saw *He Got Game*—I wanted to *be* Jesus Shuttlesworth. I definitely had people approach me from time to time asking if I needed anything. And what 16-year-old kid doesn't want to have his pockets stuffed with money?

One time during the summer before my senior year, after a long day of playing ball at Spring Lake Park, in the next town over, a bunch of us were going for beverages at 7-Eleven. A guy named Eddie was hanging with us. He had started to come around regularly, even though he must've been at least ten years older. I thought nothing of it until that day.

He had given us a ride to the store in his gray Lexus ES sedan, and while everyone else was getting out, he grabbed my arm and said, "Let me holla at you for a sec." I was in the passenger seat opposite him.

"Yo, you know you are blowing up right now?" I just looked at him, nodding my head, waiting for him to get to the point.

He then discussed how he could help with anything I needed. Money, women, flights, etc.

"Whatever it is, *we* got you."

He then reached behind me and grabbed a small duffel from under my seat. I knew I should've bolted right then and there, but my curiosity got the better of me. He placed the bag on my lap and unzipped it, and my eyes almost popped out of my head. Money. A shitload of money. Countless wads of hundreds held together by rubber bands. He reached, grabbed a stack, and held it up.

"All this is yours. We are going to rep you when the time comes, and we are about to change the game."

He then handed me the stack. I sat there wondering how much money that one wad was. I had never seen a hundred-dollar bill before. Now I had at least 40 or 50 of them in my hand. I remember thinking how wrong it was to accept it, but I sure as hell wanted to take it. My mind started racing. I could buy a whole lot of FUBU and a two-way pager.

It was 1998.

I remember thinking how soft I was being for not taking the cash.

Eddie was a "runner," which meant he did his best to recruit kids like me to be represented by an agency. And if he was successful, like so many of them are, he would get a slice of the 4 percent commission the agent received from negotiating the NBA player contract.

The truth is, it was a lot easier for me to walk away than it would've been for another kid whose parents weren't working to make ends meet. My parents were really clear with me that we were okay and that we didn't need any kind of help. They were always adamant about not letting money influence our decisions.

There's something seriously wrong with a process that puts kids in that kind of position and then brands them as cheaters if the temptation is too great for them to resist. And so I didn't look down on others who made a different decision, and I still don't to this day. Step in their shoes and then judge.

Schools weren't offering me gym bags of money. They dealt in a different currency: minutes. Coaches from all over would guarantee a starting position as soon as I walked in the door. That meant a lot of playing time right out of the gate to showcase yourself for the next level. But I knew better than to trust anybody who guaranteed something that they could just as easily be offering up to another player in the next phone call.

All I knew was I wanted to play in Chapel Hill. I had played in the Bob Gibbons Tournament of Champions, an AAU contest, in the Dean Dome and was enamored with the arena. Dean Smith had been sending me letters, but he retired at the end of my junior year and Bill Guthridge became the new coach. Shortly thereafter, I received a call from Guthridge explaining that they were dropping me off the recruiting list. They had just signed Ronald Curry from Hampton, Virginia, who was a beast. According to *USA Today*, he was the best high school football player in the country two years running, and if that wasn't impressive enough, he was also the MVP of the 1998 McDonald's All American Game. And with their point guard Ed Cota having two years of eligibility left, there wasn't enough room on the roster.

My heart sank when Guthridge delivered the news. He couldn't have been nicer, but I was fuming. I couldn't believe North Carolina was passing on me. It was pouring rain outside, but I went out anyway and shot what felt like a thousand jumpers. Fuck UNC.

I did mention I was spiteful back then.

Despite my disappointment, I consoled myself with the possibility of joining my friends at Rutgers. Dahntay Jones had committed there, and 6'10" power forward Troy Murphy of the Delbarton School, in New Jersey, was close to committing. I knew we had the potential to make some serious noise. I liked the coach, Kevin Bannon, and realized that this was an opportunity to stay local and put Rutgers on the map. So just like that, I made my decision. Or so I thought.

My parents have always lived by the notion that if you say you're going to do something, you see it through. Once you've committed to someone or something, there is no backing out. Prior to making my decision about going to Rutgers, I had scheduled a trip down south to meet with Duke's coach, Mike Krzyzewski.

"As a family, we keep our word," my dad said. "You're going to go down there, and that's final."

I protested the entire drive down. There was a forecast for a big storm, and I prayed that the weather would force us to cancel or that we'd be derailed by a flat tire.

It was the longest nine and a half hours of my life. I remember going through Virginia and thinking, *Oh my God, Virginia is the longest state ever.* For endless, tedious miles on I–95, I just stared out the window, watching tree after tree after tree, trying to get to a school I didn't even want to attend.

But when we finally got there and I walked through the doors into Cameron Indoor Stadium for the first time, my disposition completely changed. The place had a special feel to it. I'd seen a few of their games on TV, but I had never been there to experience it in person. I never had the chance to feel it. My parents and I walked into the dimly lit gym and looked up at the rafters. There, hanging down, were the 1991 and 1992 championship banners. I could feel every hair follicle on the back of my neck start to stand up. I know my mom and dad felt the same. You could almost *hear* the history just by looking at the stands that the "Cameron Crazies" have called home for so many years.

The Dean Dome didn't have a fraction of the character that Cameron Indoor had. From the outside, Cameron looked sedate. I thought I was walking into a library. Truly. There were a couple of spotlights on the banners overhead, and there was Grant Hill's retired jersey. Laettner's. Hurley's. I breathed it all in. All of these big-time names played here, in this quaint, intimate "theater."

At the time, Coach K's office was in the back corner of the gymnasium. As we walked into his office, the first thing that came to my mind was how small it was, especially considering *whose* office it was. But it was his, all right.

Both of the national championship trophies sat on top of a cabinet, with the game nets draped over each. There were pictures from the dynasty years, the '92 Dream Team, Coach K with Johnny Dawkins and Tommy Amaker. Memorabilia of all kinds. There was one picture in particular that struck me. It was of Steve "Wojo" Wojciechowski on the cover of *Sports Illustrated* with his arms crossed, staring down the camera. Only Coach K would be able to take a role player to such heights.

His desk had a commanding, grandfather-like chair behind it that dwarfed our chairs opposite him. As if meeting the man wasn't going to be intimidating enough.

So the three of us sat there . . . waiting.

Then the office door opened and we popped up out of our tiny chairs to greet him.

"Mr. Williams," he said with piercing eye contact as he shook my hand. He then shifted his full attention to my parents. "David. Althea."

It just might've been the first time I had ever been referred to as *Mr.* And what made it that much more powerful was his choosing to call my parents by their first names. He seemed taller in person. He had jet-black hair, perfectly combed—nothing's changed 17 years later—and left the lingering scent of a masculine aftershave behind. He was wearing their team warm-up suit with sneakers that looked like they came fresh out of the box. All Nike. I was transfixed.

I had never scoped out a man like this before.

Rather than sitting behind his desk, he pulled up another chair to level the playing field. After breaking the ice, talking about our trip down, the area, and such, Coach K switched gears. He talked about his background, from playing at Army under Bobby Knight to eventually coaching there, and ultimately how he ended up at Duke. What the expectations and responsibilities that came along with being a Duke player and a Duke student meant.

I wish I could recall for you everything he said, but there came a point when I saw his lips moving without hearing a sound. The whole experience felt like a dream. One thing I do remember was that my dad kept calling him Mike, which was so awkward!

The things that Coach K offered me were values—values that were already in line with the ones instilled in me by my parents. He said he wanted to sharpen them.

"I can't promise you're going to be an NBA player," he told me. "I'm not going to promise you you're going to start. I'm not going to promise you that you're going to play 25 minutes a night. But I do promise you that by the time you leave here, you will be a better man and you will learn how to approach this game in the same way that you should approach life."

It resonated with me. No one affiliated with basketball had ever discussed themes like that. Other coaches would say, "You're going to come in your freshman year, play 25 minutes . . . I can promise you this, I can promise you that . . ." and here was Coach K with his out-of-the-box thinking about becoming a man. He talked about putting me on the right path toward being successful in life.

He added that he came from the old school where being on time is being late—that you should be here early and should stay afterwards. Mediocrity would not be rewarded, so if you came here, you were coming here to be the best.

Music to my dad's ears.

It was just the type of challenge I was looking for. At a program like Duke, I would have to scrap and claw for playing time.

At the time, they had seven or eight McDonald's All Americans on the team, many of whom could potentially be there the following year. They were absolutely loaded, having just completed a 32–4 season in which they finished as conference

champions and fell in the Elite Eight to Kentucky, who went on
to win it all that year. William Avery was going into his sophomore year, and everyone expected a breakout campaign from
him at the point guard spot. Elton Brand and Shane Battier were
also going into their second year. The "Alaskan Assassin," Trajan
Langdon, was returning for his senior season. And if that wasn't
enough, they now had Chicago's pride and joy, Corey Maggette,
as an incoming freshman.

After a while, my parents decided to go on a short tour to
allow me some one-on-one time with Coach K.

"What's your goal?" he asked. I was stumped. I had an answer—
to perhaps get a college degree and play in the NBA—but I wanted
to provide him with what I thought he wanted to hear. I chose to
not say anything for fear of saying the wrong thing.

"The school gets so much from you," he said. "What are *you*
using the school for?" I instinctively said, "An education." He
followed that up by explaining how an education is one of the
priorities, but to think about the relationships this school offers.
And how to leverage those into something bigger than basketball. Basketball is just a small window, and that's assuming I was
lucky enough to have a professional career. It would be 15 years
at best, and then what? What would the plan be after that? He
emphasized how important it would be to utilize the connections
I would forge to my advantage over the long haul.

I was blown away. I was a 16-year-old kid being talked to like
a grown up. Being challenged to think about my future as a man
would.

I wasn't sold completely just yet. After all, only hours before, I
had pretty much decided to play for Rutgers.

I had developed this spiel after a while that neutralized any pressure a coach put on me about committing to their program. I would say something along the lines of "I love this. It's awesome, and it's an amazing opportunity to be down here. After we see the campus and meet some of the guys, I'm going to go back to New Jersey and take some time to weigh all this stuff out and see where things lie. You know, get my parents' input, stuff like that."

It was a good, well-rehearsed routine. But here's the brilliance of Coach K. He let me recite my lines, and when I was finished he said . . . nothing. It was like one of those awkward pauses where you don't know if you should jump back in and say something or wait to see if he's going to say something first.

Then came this gem.

"Well, look, we want you here. I want you here. But if you're not interested in Duke, then this is something I need to know, because I'm probably going to take this other kid, Todd, from New Jersey."

Oh, hell, no.

I knew exactly who he was talking about. Todd Billet played at an all-boys high school in southern New Jersey called Christian Brothers Academy. People were always saying how much better Todd was than me. Todd was ranked higher than I was in the New Jersey papers. Todd got invited to the ABCD Camp; I didn't. We had beaten Christian Brothers a couple of times, and people still said he was better than me. It drove me crazy. I'd been competing with him throughout high school, and here I was again, it seemed, competing with him for a spot on Duke.

This was the genius of Mike Krzyzewski. He first appealed to my intelligence, then to my maturity, and when I was still on the fence, he took one little jab at my vanity, and that closed the deal. I walked out of his office thinking there was no way in hell

I was going to lose my spot here to Todd Billet. And it wasn't something I was losing at all—I was Coach K's first choice—but somehow it felt like a competition. He read me like an open book and pushed the right button.

I walked out of the office into the gymnasium and saw my dad sitting on a bench next to the scorer's table, deep in thought as he stared at the retired jerseys hanging down from the rafters.

It was at that moment that I began to hear the crowd roaring, visualizing Coach K on the sideline yelling out instructions to me as I brought the ball up the court.

I walked over to where my father was sitting.

"Dad, I think we should commit."

"Jason, I'm going to go ahead and say this. I love Coach Bannon, and Rutgers is a great school. But the question I have for you is a question I have been trying to answer for about the past ten minutes. Would you rather be a king among men or a king among kings?"

"I would rather be a king among kings, Dad."

"Then, son, I don't know a better place for you than right here. This is where you will get the best education, and you will have no better mentor than that man right there."

He then told me to look up at the rafters and continued. "I know your number is 32, but you can't wear 32 here, because it's retired." It had been Laettner's number. "But if you notice, it feels like there's a missing link. You see, 11 is retired, 33 is retired, 44 is retired, but 22 is not up there. That's the missing link. You should come here to play, get the number 22 retired, and take your place as a king among kings."

And that's how I ended up at Duke.

5

Freshman

●

Women, parties, booze, and freedom from my parents were all waiting for me down in Durham.

When I landed at Greensboro airport to start the next chapter of my life, an enormous 6'9", 265 pound man-child was waiting in a beat-up red Ford Taurus to pick me up for our one-hour drive to campus. The driver's seat was pushed all the way back and the seat was reclined so Carlos Boozer's head wouldn't be scrunched against the roof. You just don't see people that big every day, much less someone of that size who can do everything I could on the court. He was just as good as I was at passing, shooting threes, and doing all the ball-handling drills. We had met months earlier at the McDonald's All American Game. I liked him from the start.

"Booz" and I talked all the way to Durham, wondering what basketball was going to be like with Coach K. Four key players from the team that had just lost to UConn in the finals would not be returning. Three of them were declaring for the draft early. The Bulls took Elton Brand with the first pick in the draft and Trajan Langdon went to the Cavs at pick 11, while Corey Maggette and William Avery went 13th and 14th, to Seattle and Minnesota, respectively. (Maggette was then traded to Orlando.)

Back then, it was strange to see Coach K lose underclassmen to the NBA. I mean, it never happened. Personally, I was shocked when Avery declared, leaving his starting spot vacant. I'd been sure I was going to end up fighting to earn my minutes, and now the show was mine.

As a result, we wondered how this mass exodus was going to blow back on us. If and when the time came, would Coach K not let us leave? That wasn't a big concern for me coming in, since I had a lot of work ahead, given that I was going to be learning a position I never played in high school. Carlos, on the other hand, expected to be at Duke for two, maybe three years tops.

"Is he going to change your game?" Boozer asked me. "Because you're a point guard, but you're not really a point guard."

That was something that was on my mind, too. I was always more of a scorer than a playmaker. Now I was going to be expected to run things with everyone looking over my shoulder. Look at the coaches who were on the Duke bench at the time: former All-American Johnny Dawkins, *SI* cover boy Wojo, and Coach K. What did all three have in common? Former point guards.

I'll never forget the night when Coach K came to my house with Dawkins for dinner after I had committed to Duke. We made a big batch of Polish sausage and invited my high school coach, Mark Taylor, to join us. I was so nervous to have Coach K at my house that I barely said a word throughout the dinner. My parents asked him plenty of questions about his team and his philosophies. They asked Dawkins about his experiences, and my dad wanted to know if he had had to worry about racism in the South.

Meanwhile, Coach was there to talk about expectations and the transition from high school to college ball. When Mike Krzyzewski talks, you listen. He is intimidating and comforting at the same time. He has a presence unlike anyone else. He was talking about how and why players like Wojo and Bobby Hurley had succeeded as PGs. All the while, Coach Taylor is rocking back in his chair, shaking his head.

Finally, Coach K looked at Coach Taylor and asked, "What do you think?" Now, Coach Taylor is one of the most headstrong individuals I have ever met—a competitive ex-athlete who led Fordham to a MAAC championship—with a lot of bravado and never shy about sharing his opinion.

Mark responded, "Can I call you Mike? I'll call you Mike. Listen, Jason isn't really a point guard. He's a two or a three, a slasher."

Everyone's jaw dropped to the floor. Was he really telling this legendary coach what's what?

Expressionless, Coach K firmly replied, "No, he's not. He's the top point guard in the country. You should use him that way."

"Let's agree to disagree," Mark said.

I guess Booz and my high school coach were on the same page about me, and we were just going to have to see how that transition was going to work.

We kept talking the whole way down, so excited about what was ahead. Chris Carrawell was going to be the only senior on the team; how would we get along with him? Junior forward Shane Battier was just so damn smart—would we even be able to have conversations with him? We talked about winning championships, going to different parties, and then storming Chapel Hill and taking their girls, too.

It was a requirement that we live on East Campus our freshman year with all the other "frosh." We didn't have the exclusive dorms that student-athletes are afforded today. I shared a corner room with Booz, and it was hysterical seeing his 6'9" frame attempting to sleep in a bed made for someone 6'0" at most. Our fellow freshman teammates suffered along with Booz. Mike Dunleavy, Casey Sanders, and Nick Horvath were 6'6", 6'11", and 6'10", respectively.

Coach K demanded we report earlier than everyone else, in July, to get settled in and begin our conditioning program. But we weren't allowed to move into the dorms yet, so Booz and I had to stay in off-campus housing for a month. Two of our upperclassman teammates—Ryan Caldbeck and Matt Christensen—were kind enough to let us use their apartment about a mile away. They were back home for the summer. Every day, we'd raid their closets and help ourselves to their Duke game shorts, rocking their gear around campus in the blistering July heat.

Months before my arrival, I received this massive book in the mail from Will Stephens, Duke's strength-and-conditioning coach. It outlined all the exercises I was supposed to do—stretches, warm-ups, cardio drills, stuff like that. But like a typical teenager I just skimmed it, thinking, *I just got done with high school. I need a break.*

That training manual collected dust for two months. I spent the summer hanging out with friends, getting ready to live the dream, thinking I had it down. They gave us a couple of days to get acclimated, then Booz and I met with the head manager, Jeff LaMere, and his staff, who'd be supervising our workouts. Their job was to coordinate our practices, prepare all of our equipment in the locker rooms and on the court, remind us of our individual workout times, and basically coordinate the whole show.

Will Stephens told Carlos and me that our first workout would be on the track. Now, if you've never been to North Carolina in July, let me tell you, it is not the most comfortable place in the world. It's 100 degrees and the humidity is off the charts. You're dripping sweat just from walking. Booz had just eaten two or three hot dogs and was finishing the last one as we walked into the locker room. Jeff said, "Boozer, having hot dogs before a workout is probably not the best thing to do."

Carlos, a gentle giant off the court, had a chip on his shoulder back then. "Whatever, Jeff. I'm good." We got dressed, put on our blue shorts with the Duke logo, and began to officially commence our college basketball careers. When we went outside, we noticed all of the skill-position players of the football team warming up. Will told us we would be working out with them. And that was when it occurred to me how smart it would've been to have opened that thick book.

One drill had us running around the track, and every time we hit a certain mark, we had to do a sprint. I don't know how many meters, but it was a long-distance sprint. We jogged, then sprinted, then jogged, then sprinted—15 or 20 times. I'd never worked out like this before. The heat was unbearable.

After doing these jog-sprints, I was ready to keel over and pass out. After four, I almost threw up in my mouth. So if I'm struggling, how do you think poor Boozer is doing? He's from Alaska. There's no heat like this in Alaska. He sounded like a wounded animal. When people are tired, it's normal to put your hands on your knees and breathe heavily. His toes were pointed inward, his knees were touching, and he was taking these deep breaths that sounded like a bear moaning in the woods.

"Yo, Booz, you okay? You gonna make it?"

All he could manage was *"Mmmmmmmmmmmmmmmm."*

It's hysterical now, but at the time I was too tired to laugh. We sprinted with the wide receivers and picked up huge tractor tires and pulled ropes in the sand against each other, all this Navy SEAL shit. Afterwards, we crawled back into the locker room and into this massive bathroom, where we collapsed on the cold tile floor.

That was when Boozer threw up on himself.

Jeff was standing just outside the bathroom door with a knowing look on his face. "See, Carlos, I told you you shouldn't have had a hot dog."

"Shut the fuck up, Jeff, and go get me another dog," Boozer wheezed.

And that was just the first day. Eventually things got a little easier, but it certainly took a lot to adjust to training at that level. If you're a Duke recruit reading this right now, I have one piece of advice: read the damn book.

The first week of practices was a nightmare. I knew nothing. I couldn't remember plays, and my conditioning was still a work in progress. J.D. Simpson was guarding me; he was a junior walk-on and was in terrific shape. We were playing five-on-five, and I remember getting the ball inbounded, turning around, and almost colliding face-to-face. His defensive pressure was relentless. I wasn't even able to bring the ball up the floor. He never got tired.

"Stop!" Coach K barked when I turned the ball over. "Why would you do that? Why would you go this way? Why didn't you just beat him up the court? Beat him up the court!" And he would do this little driving motion with his right hand where he would rock his fist back and forth like he was steering the top of an imaginary wheel, while yelling, "Drive him up the court!"

In the very beginning, I was discouraged and would put my head down. It took me a while to understand that he wasn't attacking me but rather challenging me.

I finally beat J.D. up the court and tried to get us into a set, but I was dead tired and could barely gather my breath, let alone my thoughts. I'd never played at such a frantic pace. It was exponentially faster than anything I was used to, but it was normal for a Coach K team.

We went through the routine countless times, each time with Coach yelling out new instructions. "Now beat him with your left." "No! You're going too fast; slow down." "Change speeds." I didn't even know what changing speeds meant. In high school, I was able to do things athletically that other people couldn't.

I struggled handling multiple instructions at once. He even took it to the next level by giving me hand signals. How the hell am I supposed to get the ball up the court, communicate with you, focus on the defender, get us in a set, and catch my breath all at the same time?!

"God dammit, Jason, *look at me!*"

After each practice, I just sat at my locker with my hands massaging my cranium, quietly panicking.

There's no way I'm going to make it here. There's no way I'm cut out for this type of shit. If I'd gone to Rutgers, I would have been able to do what I wanted to do. Did I pick the wrong place to come to school?

It was comforting knowing that I wasn't alone. This was a first for all of us. Boozer, Dunleavy, Casey Sanders, Nick Horvath— we all went through the "spin cycle" together.

I spent the entire year playing catch-up. I was constantly

"chasing the rabbit," learning how to process information at warp speed. I never did so many things on the fly in my life. It was like someone saying to you, "Hey, you've never been a CEO before, but we want you to come and run IBM."

I wasn't used to a coach grabbing me by the collar of my jersey and being in my face. Or being in a film session where the tape always seemed to freeze to pinpoint something I'd done wrong. There would be 20 or so people in the room, and a Hall of Fame coach would direct his pointer to the screen as everyone watched in horror to see where the red dot was going to land. More often than not, it found its way to the point guard.

Jason, you're not buying into what we're trying to achieve defensively. Your hands are on your knees five minutes into the game. Are you tired? Shane just fell down right next to you. Why didn't you pick him up? Never bend at the knees for a loose ball. Dive, Jason!

Coach K wasn't the only one challenging me in front of everyone. Shane Battier had no reservations about doing the same. After pretty much every play in practice—games, too—he would get the team in a huddle. It didn't take long before I gravitated to Shane whenever we were on the court together. He was the smartest player I'd ever met, and he was all of two years older than me. He would remember things I had to do on top of his own assignments.

During a home game against UNC that season, there was a break in the action, and Shane rounded us up. It was loud as hell. He then laid right into me, saying, "Jay, why in the hell do you keep letting Ed Cota go right? *You* know the scouting report says he prefers to drive right. Force him left, and if he beats you, I got you! Let's *go*!"

None of us who know Shane from those days are surprised with how things ended up for him after Duke. He just concluded a 13-year run in the NBA that featured two championship rings and a list of accolades that can go on for pages.

If Shane was the vocal leader of the team, Chris Carrawell was our quiet closer. He was the only senior on the team, and he'd been waiting for his turn. The year before, he had taken a backseat to guys like Brand and Maggette. Now, Chris was bailing us out time after time with one clutch bucket after another.

I was always thinking on the court my freshman year. I didn't stop thinking and start reacting until my sophomore year.

We started off the season by losing our first two games in the Coaches vs. Cancer Classic in Madison Square Garden. In my first Duke game ever, in front of my hometown crowd, we lost to Stanford when I air-balled a three-pointer that would've tied the game with seconds left in overtime.

My stat line was abysmal: *3-for-15 from the field, 3 assists, 6 turnovers, 13 points.*

Not exactly the homecoming I was hoping for. I was quoted in the Duke *Chronicle* saying, "I've got to wake up and smell the coffee." Coach K had my back in the postgame presser. "He's got a lot to learn to become an outstanding point guard, but he has the guts and talent and just has to learn the position. His first game was in Madison Square Garden. That's a big classroom."

The next game was a rematch of the NCAA final the year before against UConn. This time around, however, neither team resembled anything close to the powerhouse they were only months earlier. I led the team with just 16 points and got absolutely obliterated by Khalid El-Amin. I never thought someone so pudgy could be so damn quick and deceptive at the same time. My conditioning was nowhere near where it needed to be.

Coach K told me, "You're going to start riding the bike for

45 minutes and watching tape with Wojo every day after practice." Steve Wojciechowski was—and still is to this day—the most
passionate guy I've ever been around when it comes to basketball.
Wojo was the epitome of the player who left everything on the
court. He didn't possess the athletic gifts that the rest of us had and
he knew it, which made him outwork everyone. Rudy Ruettiger
had nothing on him. He created a trend that you still see to this day
where players slap the floor on defense when they need a stop. Even
now it takes me back when I watch him coach Marquette, and have
fits on the sideline. He cares *that* much about each possession.

The stationary bike was in the media room, right smack in
front of the projector. Wojo sat right next to me as I was hauling
ass on the bike. He would set the clock for 45 minutes. The bike
was on an incline, which had me out of the seat in a standing position like I was Lance Armstrong trying to climb a mountain—
minus the PEDs.

I'm riding, he's talking, and we're both watching tape. At his
discretion, he'd stop the tape, put me through a quick Q&A,
and then fast-forward to the next possession. He kept telling me,
"You have to train yourself to think while you're tired." And he
was relentless. It was a one-sided conversation that went like this:

*He jumped on the high side of the ball screen; how should you have
attacked it? Should you have bumped him? Why are you going 8,000
miles an hour? Why don't you slow down and go 20? . . . This is
where you need to burst! Look at when Shane's man steps up—that's
when you attack. . . . Why not give him a bounce pass? Why would
you throw a lob? You know Carlos is tired; look at Carlos's face. Why
aren't you talking to Carlos during the time-out? Why aren't you telling
him to sprint the floor? . . . Look, why aren't you talking to Chris right
here? Coach is trying to talk to you, and you walk away. . . . Why are*

you not looking at the coaches on the bench? Why are you not down in the stance? Why are you half-assing it?

This was my version of pledging a fraternity. I think about those days on the bike, dissecting tape, more than playing in actual games my freshman year, because those days were way harder than the game ever was.

And that's exactly the point.

Of all the things Coach K taught me about basketball, learning how to play through mistakes was the most important of all. Of course, I didn't pick up on that right away. And it definitely didn't help my confidence that K had no problem pointing out all my mistakes, either. There wasn't accountability in high school—the focus was on all of us as a unit, not the individual. And when K called you out, he'd put you on an island regardless of your accolades.

"You're going to be evaluated by what you do *after* the mistake instead of what got you in the position to make that mistake."

After those first two losses, we won 18 in a row.

Near the end of the regular season, we were playing St. John's at Cameron Indoor Stadium. At the time, they were loaded; I'd played against a bunch of them in those Riverside Church games growing up. They had Erick Barkley, Lavor Postell, and Bootsy Thornton, who had scorched Duke at MSG the year before I arrived. I was at that game my senior year in high school and saw Thornton drop 40 on them.

I was having one of my better performances, and Shane was in a good rhythm, too. Bootsy had just hit a jumper to put them up by one with ten seconds left, and I immediately took the inbounds pass, sprinted the ball past half-court, and called a time-out with about five seconds left. During the time-out, Coach K drew up a play.

The lineup was Shane, Chris, Nate James, Boozer, and me. Carrawell was the inbounds passer; Nate was stationed at the bottom left-hand corner, outside the three-point line; Booz down low on the left block; Shane centered just above the three-point line; and I was positioned at the right elbow. I was to come off a screen set by Shane to catch the inbounds pass from Chris. Shane's assignment was to then immediately headhunt my man and set another screen for me at the top of the key, leaving the entire right side of the court open. If he did this successfully, I would have a bevy of options. I could find Shane rolling to the basket just after he set the screen, or come off the screen and take the shot myself if I had space.

"Jason, either this is your jump shot, you attack the rim, or you get Shane the ball and let Shane finish the play," K said. "We're going to win this game."

And he meant it. After drawing up the play, he started giving instructions on what to do on defense after the shot went in.

"Jason, force Barkley to his left and turn him a couple of times before he gets to half-court. Everybody else, we are in our 21 defense."

We put our hands together in the huddle and K repeated, "We're going to win." We yelled, "One, two, three, *Duke!*" I hadn't felt more confident the entire year than at that moment walking back on the court. I knew we were going to win. The noise in the building was intoxicating.

And then it happened.

I'm a stride behind Carrawell and Booz coming out of the huddle when I notice C-Well tap his shoulder and say, "Pop out, man, pop out and just give the ball right back to me."

I didn't just hear what I thought I did, right? Then I saw Booz nod back to him as they exchanged a quick fist bump.

This couldn't be happening. No way in hell were they going against K's plan. That would be sacrilegious.

The ref then handed C-Well the ball as we all stood in our designed positions. As Shane came down to set a screen for me, sure enough, there's Booz breaking his assignment and flashing toward C-Well. Chris then threw Booz the ball and got it right back once he stepped inbounds. Coming off the screen, I dropped my shoulders in disgust as I looked over to Coach K, watching the play unfold in disbelief. C-Well then attempted to go one-on-one, taking an ill-advised 15-footer that didn't look good the moment it left his hands.

Game over.

No one said a word to each other as we made our way back to the locker room. I was so shocked about what had just happened that the loss itself didn't even register. We were just sitting there with our heads down when Coach K entered the room, looking baffled. I'd seen him angry at times, but this was different. This was more like a parent being disappointed with his child. He just kept pacing back and forth, not making eye contact with anyone, softly muttering to himself just loud enough for us to hear.

"I don't know why you guys wouldn't listen to me. Why you wouldn't trust me. I know what I'm doing."

He then stopped on a dime and locked in on Booz.

"Why did you do that, Carlos? Why?" K started.

Carlos didn't know what to say.

That was when C-Well stepped up: "I told him to do it. I changed the play, I told Boozer to pop out, and I told him to give me the ball."

Coach K looked genuinely wounded. His lone senior, who had been with him the longest and whom he trusted the most, had defied an order. It was an act of betrayal. K usually stood with his body upright, but at that moment he looked as if somebody had ripped his soul out and snapped it into pieces.

"I have never had a player not trust me. I'm so hurt that you did that. I'm not only hurt, but your teammates are hurt, because you didn't trust in them."

That was all he said.

We all looked at C-Well. He got the point. We all got the point. No individual was bigger than the team. Other coaches might have waited to speak with C-Well alone, or lost their cool and chastised him in front of the rest of his peers. Not K. It was important to him that we all understood this error of judgment, in order for us *all* to move forward as *one*.

We assumed it was over. Point taken. Time to move on.

But this is Coach K we're talking about.

The next day at practice he addressed us. "Chris, you should apologize to the team. And you guys should decide whether you want to forgive Chris or not. Because some things you do in this life aren't forgivable. They're not. And if that's one of the things that you guys think is forgivable, then you guys need to come together and talk about it." He then left us to talk.

Chris stood up. "Look, this is my last year, and I've been waiting for moments like that my entire career, and I felt hurt because I didn't know if Coach trusted me to step up. I'm sorry."

At that moment we got to know the real Chris Carrawell, insecurities and all. He had been stepping up for us all year, and now here he was, apologizing to everyone for letting them down. Imagine a senior saying he was sorry to a bunch of freshmen. It made us want to fight for him.

And such was the brilliance of Mike Krzyzewski. He knew

that the night before, we'd ended up being okay with C-Well and Booz on the surface. That we *could* move on from that loss. But that wasn't nearly enough if we were to become special. We needed to be more than just "okay" with one another. It was just primer. So the next morning, he went about adding another coat of paint to solidify things for our future.

We went from being *cool* to happily taking a bullet for one another.

We didn't lose another game the rest of the regular season. We did win the ACC tournament and the conference championship that year.

Toward the end of the regular season, UNC's Joe Forte had been named the ACC Rookie of the Year. That day in practice, I remember Coach K telling me how I would be recognized as the best college freshman in the *country* once I lit up the ACC and NCAA tournaments, like he was sure I would.

"I *know* it," K said, "And I just want you to know that."

We would go on to win the ACC tournament and were one of the favorites for the national championship until Mike Miller and the Florida Gators knocked us out in the Sweet Sixteen 87–78. I played like shit that night and still blame myself for the loss.

Later that spring, after "The Flintstones" of Michigan State won the title, I was named national Freshman of the Year by *The Sporting News*.

All in all, it was a tough year. I was exhausted. *But* I was also inspired. I decided to stay in Durham for the summer, take some courses, work out every day, and build on everything I'd learned. Coach K knew big things were in store for me.

For a while, I wasn't sure. I'd spent the whole year playing catch-up, unaware of how far I had come.

My eyes were opening.

6

Duke

•

Basketball isn't basketball without some good old-fashioned trash talking.

I found my alter ego that summer in a gym at the Lahaina Civic Center, in Maui. I was in Hawaii for the USA Men's Under–21 team practices. Team USA was also in town, preparing for the Summer Olympics in Sydney, only months away, where they would win the gold medal. We practiced daily against the likes of Ray Allen, Vince Carter, Kevin Garnett, Tim Hardaway, Alonzo Mourning, and Jason Kidd. As confident as I was at the time, competing against these greats was a major learning experience, particularly when it came to expressing myself on the court. I got trounced in a trash-talking duel with the great Gary Payton. *The Glove.*

All my life, I had been a "quiet" basketball player who never responded to trash talk. That is, until I faced the only point guard ever to win the NBA Defensive Player of the Year Award. In our first scrimmage against them, I was left wide-open for a shot in the left-hand corner of the court. As I elevated, out of the corner of my eye I saw G.P. running at me full-speed for what I thought was an attempt to block my shot. I instinctively adjusted, bracing myself for what was to come. But he never left his feet. Instead he balled his right hand into a fist and bumped my private area.

I was speechless.

I later learned that this was not an uncommon trick in the NBA, but at the time I was absolutely infuriated. I ended up shooting an air ball that led to an outlet pass from Kidd to Garnett for a two-handed tomahawk. As I brought the ball up the court on the next possession, G.P. was staring directly at me while he backpedaled toward the half-court line, his head swaying from side to side with a level of arrogance I had never seen in an opponent before. He proceeded to call me every name in the book, talking loud enough so that everyone in the gym could hear exactly what he was saying.

"I got this little runt. He ain't shit. He ain't gonna do nothing. He gonna cough it up. He don't know who he dealin' with. Little bitch-ass dude from Duke. This ain't Duke, you Dooookie. Coach K make y'all soft down there, huh?"

All of a sudden he blitzed me at half-court, forcing me to my left while hanging all over my right shoulder. Then he forcefully jumped to my left side to go for the steal, causing me to spin to keep possession. By the time I completed the move, the ball was *gone.* I looked down at my right hand expecting the ball to be there, but instead it was at the other end, being finger-rolled into the basket by the Glove.

"I told ya. I told ya. Soft-ass Dooooookiiiiieeee."

On the next possession, I made sure to dish the ball off the second I got over half-court. Later on that same play, I found myself open in the corner for a three.

And there he was . . . again.

He closed in on me and extended his arm. This time I quickly shot the ball and swung my arms down toward him as strongly as possible. My forearms cracked right into his hands. By the grace of God the shot went in, and as I backpedaled down the court with him still hanging on me, I uttered the worst piece of trash talk imaginable.

You ain't the Glove. You're the mitten.

His look said it all. I should've apologized to him on the spot and begged him not to repeat what I just said. As the game went on, he lured me into playing his way and not mine. I began to speak like him. Curse after curse after curse, regardless of how a play unfolded. There was no rhyme or reason; it became a game within the game.

The old me, five minutes earlier, would've quietly bitched to himself.

Now I was vocal. I never looked back.

I credit G.P. for helping me find out who I really was as a player.

After a week and change in Hawaii, we left for Brazil for the 2000 COPABA World Championship. I was 18 at the time, hormones raging, feeling great about myself, and here I was in a foreign country looking at the most beautiful women I had ever seen. It felt like I was living in a music video.

We played the tournament in a small city near São Paulo called Ribeirão Preto, which is dubbed the "Brazilian California." It was there that I turned a corner as a player. I had the good fortune to play with so many future stars, like Zach Randolph and Jason Richardson out of Michigan State, Arkansas's Joe Johnson, and

Tayshaun Prince out of Kentucky, to name a few. I led the team in points, assists, and three-pointers made, shooting 56 percent from the field and 62 percent from downtown. I mean, I played out of my mind that week.

Jim Boeheim was our head coach, and Jay Wright, then the head coach at Hofstra, was our assistant. Boeheim was already a legend at Syracuse, and Wright is doing great things today as the head coach at Villanova. I really liked both of them right off the bat. They had a similar coaching style that was quite different from Coach K's approach. It took a while for me to feel comfortable with K, and maybe, looking back, it was because he was so damn intimidating. I instantly felt at ease with Jim and Jay, like they were my friends, not authority figures like Coach K.

As my game took off to new heights, my self-confidence grew along with it. There were no bed checks, overbearing coaches, or upperclassmen monitoring us on that trip. So I did what any normal 18-year-old young man would've done given the chance. The first night, I went out late with some of the guys, drinking, smoking weed, and hooking up with gorgeous Brazilian girls. The next day, I'd play incredibly well, and I'd go back out for round two. Instead of my play suffering from all the late-night extracurricular activities, it elevated. So it was justifiable to keep enjoying myself.

Round three . . . four . . . five . . .

My off-season was shaping up beautifully. Everything seemed to fall into place. When I got back to Durham, though, it was all business. I spent every day working to make a mandatory 500 shots, at least two to three hundred of them from NBA three-point range. It began to feel so natural. And while my attitude toward others never changed—I remained respectful and kind to everyone—I knew that on the court, it was never going to be the same again. In just the last month, I had experienced so many firsts. I'd gone toe-to-toe with G.P., J-Kidd, Vinsanity, K.G., Ray Allen (a.k.a. Jesus Shuttlesworth) . . . I'd played the best basketball of my life with our country's name across my chest. J-Rich and I talked about what life would be like at the next level—something I had never broached up until that point. I mean, I never had the nerve to use "when" instead of "if" when it came to that subject. My confidence was off the charts.

I wasn't the only one who improved from year to year. Our core for that upcoming season was impressive, and the media agreed, ranking us No. 2 in the preseason, behind Gilbert Arenas, Richard Jefferson, and the rest of the Arizona Wildcats. After winning ACC Player of the Year and being named a first-team All-American, C-Well was drafted by the Spurs in the second round that summer. Mike Dunleavy, unfortunately, had spent most of his first year battling mono, but now he was healthy, a couple of inches taller and 20 pounds bulkier. Booz had gotten cut by the under–21 USA team—the same one Dunleavy and I had just played for—and literally had a "gut check" about his physical conditioning, so he'd worked his ass off the entire summer. Shane, who was already the best defender in college ball, finally had his offense catch up to his defense. Our glue guy, Nate James, was back for his senior year, ready to play the part of unspoken leader.

And then . . . there was . . . Chris Duhon.

Where do I begin with my boy Chris?

My freshman year, before I ever played my first game for Duke, I met this skinny, baby-faced-looking kid from Slidell, Louisiana, who was in town on a recruiting trip. Chris was a senior in high school at the time, and had narrowed his search to either us or Kentucky. He was rated the top point guard in the country, which made me wary from the jump. I remember Coach K pulling me aside earlier that day, discussing his vision for Chris and me to be the next dynamic duo just like Tommy Amaker and Johnny Dawkins. But I wasn't hearing it. This was the freshman version of myself who hadn't even played a college game yet, so naturally I was skeptical. I figured if the "Jason Williams PG experiment" didn't pan out, K would have his insurance policy in the form of future freshman Chris Duhon.

Coach decided to have Chris join our pickup games that day. I wanted him to pit us against each other so I could put the kid in his place, but K mandated that we play on the same team. The first couple of possessions, I made a point of bringing the ball up the court to show him who's in charge. A couple of plays later, we were in transition, and after blowing by my guy, I kicked the ball out to him in the corner for a three, which he knocked down effortlessly. As we were heading back on defense, he acknowledged me by saying, "Great pass, man. Let's get it going."

We ended up killing everybody out there together. Eventually, it didn't matter who brought the ball up the court, which one of us was the passer or the shooter. We just flowed, like we'd been doing this together for years. Coach K wasn't watching, but he knew already. He always did.

That night, at a party on Central Campus, the whole crew was out. Booz, Dun-Dun, Casey, Nick, our homegirl from the women's team Krista Gingrich . . . Chris was our guest for the evening. He was soft-spoken with us. I chalked it up to him being a fish out of water. But now, almost two decades and an NBA career later, he's the same old soft-spoken Chris.

He and I talked about running everyone off the court earlier that day, laughing at our instant chemistry. But after a couple of drinks, my insecurity got the better of me . . . again. This time I decided I'd show him up by drinking him under the table. I'm not sure if I grabbed a bottle of Aristocrat or Jose Cuervo— I'm positive it tasted awful—as I challenged Chris to a chugging contest. Without even waiting for a response, I put the bottle to my mouth and took a good three or four gulps without coming up for air. With a definite buzz, I passed it over to Chris, anxious to see the fear in his eyes. He calmly put his hand out, took the bottle, and began to drink. And drink. I'm not sure how much time passed before he stopped downing the bottle, but it was damn long. He then handed the bottle back to me and said, "Your turn."

Frozen, with my mouth agape, I replied, "Nah. I'm good."

And that was how it all started.

BEFORE THE SEASON, Coach gathered the team together and encouraged us to share what our dreams were for this year. Mine was to throw the ball up as high as possible, and when it came down, we would be national champions.

In our first game that season, we played Princeton at home. At one point we ran one of our basic sets, where Shane set a ball screen for me up high. The defense switched on the screen, so I was supposed to pass the ball to Shane to exploit the mismatch with a smaller player trying to stop him. But the bigger defender didn't pick me up right away, and even though I was at least a foot behind the three-point line, I took the shot without hesitation. *Splash.* I glanced over at Coach K with a look of confidence, almost defiant. A year earlier, I would've gone for the "safe" option—passing to Shane coming out of the screen.

But this wasn't last year.

One of our most memorable exploits from that year came just nine days later when we were in New York City for the preseason NIT. It was Thanksgiving eve and we had just beaten Texas in the semis the day before. We were staying at the Marriot Marquis in Times Square.

From the moment I landed, I had been exchanging texts with a girl named Noelle. She and I had met in high school when we were both playing AAU ball. I was 16 at the time. She was my first kiss—I was a late bloomer, clearly. She was now a junior on the women's basketball team at Wagner College, in Staten Island. Noelle was tall, fair-skinned, with this wild, curly hair that would fall beneath her shoulders anytime she had it straightened. She was the product of a white, Irish Catholic mother and an African American father, both from Jersey City. She was stunning.

After our Thanksgiving feast with the team, I sent a text to Noelle asking how to get to Staten Island. She didn't take me seriously but humored me anyway with the details. She was having a party that night with the rest of her team. Noelle kept challenging me, saying there was no way I'd actually travel that far to see her.

She didn't understand how much I'd changed by then.

At the dinner, I asked Chris and Andre Buckner if they wanted to roll out. It was only a week or so into the season and Chris was already my wingman, so he was always down for whatever. Andre was from Hopkinsville, Kentucky. He needed some big city fun. And so it was on.

After bed checks, at around 10:30, our clandestine mission

began. Two taxi rides and a Staten Island Ferry later, we had arrived.

From the moment we walked in the door, the party started. Chris was hanging with Noelle's roommate, Whitney, and Andre was making headway with this other girl on the team named Erin. We downed every different kind of liquor they had while playing drinking games against their men's team. I remember looking over at Chris and Dre-Buck, thinking this was the best night of their lives up to that point.

Meanwhile, I was starting to fall hard for Noelle. She and I took things to another level courtesy of that night.

To say we were drunk would be an understatement. We would've ended up missing the 4:15 A.M. ferry back to Manhattan had it not been for Noelle. We were three hot messes sitting on a rocking commuter boat, hoping the cold November air would sober us up. Chris and I both started to get seasick. Andre, apparently, was in a lot better shape, cracking jokes and doing funny impersonations. I still don't know how we were able to make it back to our rooms that morning.

The midday shootaround was a disaster for Chris and me. It would've been impossible for the coaches not to smell the alcohol coming off our bodies. I was throwing errant passes, while Chris kept dribbling the ball off his foot. We were asking for Gatorade every two minutes. Meanwhile, Andre looked like he'd slept 12 hours the night before.

"I must be coming down with the flu," I said, sweating like a pig the whole time.

Late in a very close game against Temple that night, I hit a three-pointer that put us up by just one point. Shortly after, there was this wild scramble for a loose ball. I remember diving for it, and just when I was about to grab it, a player on the other team dove on top of me, forcing the ball to roll away toward Chris. Right then he dove for it, but to no avail, as it continued to make its way toward our bench. I don't know where I got the energy, but I popped up, sprinted, jumped over Chris, and dove again. This time I was able to gather the ball and call a time-out before my momentum took me out of bounds. It turned out to be a critical play on our way to winning the preseason NIT, 63–61.

The next day, while watching tape of the game, Coach K stopped and started to point out the things we had done well, to reinforce good habits. He commended Shane for this, Nate for that. And when we got to the loose-ball fiasco that Chris and I were a part of, K played it in real speed, rewound it, replayed it in slow motion, and then paused it after I called the time-out.

"See that!" he said, shaking the pointer at the screen in approval. "What you guys did there—that won the game. Keep doing that!"

Chris and I glanced at each other, shrugging our shoulders, with a look that said, *If that's what Coach wants. . .*

Everyone considers North Carolina to be Duke's biggest rival, but from 1999 to 2002 it was Maryland. There was no place I hated playing more than Cole Field House. My roommate in Brazil the previous summer had become my archnemesis. Steve Blake ended up becoming one of Maryland's all-time great point guards, and he's still playing in the NBA all these years later. He was 6'3" with a wingspan of 6'5". He gave me some breathing room on defense, but used his length and height advantage to contest my jump shot. The media loved to hype our matchup whenever our teams met. I was essentially battling two things: Steve's incredible defense and my need to prove to him, and everyone else, that he wasn't going to stop me. And if there was a third obstacle to consider, it was their fans.

We were ranked second in the nation, and Maryland was eighth, when we met on January 27, 2001, in Cole. For the first 39 minutes, we played terribly, while the Terps played a fantastic game against us from beginning to end.

Well, almost to the end.

The pivotal moment in the game was when Steve Blake fouled out. When I saw him on the sidelines, I felt like I had a fresh chamber of oxygen to inhale. With their best defender out of the game, I became a dog off the leash.

And so began what was to become the Miracle Minute.

Down ten with a minute to go, I brought the ball upcourt, juked right at the top of the key, and drove left down the middle of the lane for an uncontested layup.

53.5 seconds left. Down by eight.

We immediately went into our 41 press, which meant full-court pressure and ball denial. Our main objective was to force their inbounds pass to the corners of the court, where the sideline and baseline could be used as extra defenders for trapping. The ball went to Drew Nicholas, and Shane and I instantly trapped him in the left corner. When Drew tried to shield the ball by putting it on the right side of his body, I swiped at it. The ball popped up off him and jumped right into my hands. My immediate reaction was to dribble once to the three-point arc and let it fly. I hadn't shot well all game, and that was the first jump shot that felt just right. In hindsight, I'm convinced I fouled him, but the ref closest to the play had his view blocked by Shane.

48.7 seconds left. Down by five.

Maryland called time-out. In our huddle, there was not much

talk, just the look in Coach K's eyes that said we were going to win. When I hit that three, everyone on our bench popped up out of their seats, revitalized, just as I had been only seconds earlier, watching Blake take a permanent seat. He drew up a play and made a substitution, putting Andre Buckner in for Dun-Dun, which gave us a smaller lineup so we could be quicker defensively and try for another steal. It seemed to backfire when Andre fouled Drew Nicholas before the ball was even inbounded, which sent Drew to the free-throw line for two shots.

Drew missed the first free throw, and this was where the plot thickened. Most people think we Dukies are altar boys, but I had taken Gary Payton's "seminar" on how best to rattle your opponent. Chris and I started talking to Drew while he was preparing for his second free throw. It was Chris's job to box out Nicholas on the line, and I was directly behind Drew, leaning forward, making sure he could hear my every word. What happened next was pure comedy.

Chris began. "Jay, this shit is coming up short."

"No way, bro, this is going way long. This mothafucka gonna brick this shit."

"Nah, his soft ass is gonna air-ball this for sure." Chris was a natural.

"Yo, when I rebound this shit, we're out," I said. "We're about to win this fucking game. Yeah, Drew. How you gonna feel when you lose this game?"

Sure enough, the shot hit the front of the rim, where Booz stretched for dear life to win the rebound. With his left hand extended, Booz tipped the ball free toward the Maryland bench, where the most athletic player on the floor—Chris Duhon—was able to chase it down. Chris grabbed the loose ball, took one drib-ble, and passed it to me.

The play Coach K had drawn up during the previous time-out was called L.A.—our high screen-and-roll series with Shane and me. It was almost impossible to stop. Shane would set a screen for me at the top of the three-point line, Dun-Dun was in the far right-hand corner, Chris in the left-hand corner, and Booz on the opposite block from where I would come off the screen. It was like being at a buffet, I had so many choices. It was every guard's dream.

Option A: If I was being guarded tightly, and my defender de-cided to go under the screen, I had the green light to shoot the ball.

Option B: If my defender tried to go over the top of the screen—squeezing between Shane and me—I would stop, dip my left shoulder into his chest, and then proceed to turn the corner and either get to the basket or draw Boozer's man to me for an easy pass and dunk.

Option C: If my defender and Shane's man decided to double-team me off the ball screen, Shane would pop to the three-point line, where I'd throw it back to him for the open shot.

Option D: If my defender was able to get over the top of the screen, he would still be a step behind as I drove to the basket, forc-ing someone—usually Dun-Dun's man or Chris's man—to help, which would leave one of them wide-open for a kick-out three.

Option E: If the defense were able to hold Shane, Chris, Dun-Dun, and me in check, then that would leave Booz on the low post for a one-on-one isolation play.

I still find it amusing that our last option was to dump the ball into a future two-time NBA All-Star.

I rushed the ball up the court like my life depended on it.

Shane and I were in lockstep—just as we had been all season long—and as I took one look at Danny Miller, I knew exactly what I was going to do next.

Every time Shane set a screen for me, it was my job to pay attention to how *his* defender would react. Shane's job was to take my defender out of the equation.

His defender was none other than Danny Miller, who'd played for the same AAU coach I did back in Jersey. I knew Danny's game well. Let's just say Danny was always more preoccupied with his offense than with his defense. Poor Coach Gary Williams didn't have as good a scouting report on his own player as I did. So as Shane set the screen, I saw Danny start to backpedal, standing straight up with his hands down by his sides. I took one dribble off the screen and elevated. Danny must've been six feet away instead of six inches. He never had a chance. I held my follow-through motion as I, and 15,000 fellow onlookers, watched the ball float through the net.

40.4 seconds left. Down by two.

Maryland called their final time-out after Tahj Holden couldn't find anyone to inbound the ball to. We sprinted over to the bench, and I sat down to catch my breath. When I looked up, everyone was huddled together, arms wrapped so tightly around one another that it felt like I was in an igloo. Coach K knelt down on his right knee and began to shout. "We're going to win this fucking game! Do you hear me?" He then slowed his speech down. "We . . . are going . . . to win . . . this fucking . . . game."

We were locked in. It was probably the only time we had ever walked back on the floor not saying a word to each other. Not even Shane had anything to add. We knew what we had to do— what we were going to do.

When Juan Dixon received the corner inbounds pass, Nate was draped all over him as Juan bobbled the ball. In a flash, Juan was triple-teamed on the sideline, directly in front of our bench, exactly where Drew Nicholas had turned the ball over a few plays earlier. Frantic, he was trying to pivot his way out of the trap when Nate went in for the steal and snagged it away. Our 41 press had paid off once again.

Nate then kicked the ball out to Chris, who waited for me to pop out from the other side of the court. I got the ball and, without hesitation, tried to attack the rim but slipped on the drive. Somehow, thankfully, I was able to maintain my dribble on one knee as I scanned the floor to find someone to bail me out. I almost threw the game away before spotting Shane open at the top. Shane took one dribble and passed it to Chris on the opposite wing behind the three-point line for a shot. With two men closing in, Chris head-faked and found Dun-Dun for an open three. He missed the shot, but our savior Nate James was there for a put-back. He missed it but got fouled on the play. Nate went to the line for two shots.

First shot . . . cash.

Second shot . . . money.

21.9 seconds left. Tie ball game.

We had managed to score 10 unanswered points in 32 seconds. Drew Nicholas missed a three-pointer from the corner at the buzzer—overtime. We ended up winning the game by two, 98–96. In our last huddle of the game, Shane was adamant about us not celebrating on their floor after the win. It was important that our opponents knew that we expected to win, no matter the circumstances.

It wasn't until the bus ride after that I found out about my mom getting hit in the stands by a glass bottle. Moments later, Chris received the same news about his mother. And Booz's mom got the worst of it when a glass bottle hit her in the head and gave her a concussion. We were livid. Ready to go back into Cole and fight. If I didn't like Maryland before, I sure as hell hated them now.

Nine games later, Maryland would have their chance, this time in our house. In the second half, Booz broke the third metatarsal in his right foot, leaving us completely exposed down low. We lost 91–80, and, to add insult to injury (no pun intended), on Shane's and Nate's Senior Night. We were completely dejected back in the locker room. Any Duke loss was treated as if there was a death in the family. Heads down. Tears. Unbearable silence. We thought our chances of winning a conference title, much less an NCAA title, had gone down the drain after getting the news that Booz would be out at least a month. That meant the soonest he'd be back was the Final Four—*if* we made it that far.

Our collective confidence was shaken even more the next day at practice. We were in the locker room getting ready to watch tape from the night before when Coach K entered. He looked resolute and energized in a room full of deflated players.

He began. "If you listen to me, we're going to win a national championship." Then, using his patented right-hand up-and-down motion, almost as if he were saluting us sideways, he slowed his speech and lowered his decibel level. "If you motherfuckers . . . listen to me . . . we're going to win a national championship." We were all ears. He explained how we were going to play "small ball." He asked Nate James if he would come off the bench so he could insert Chris into the starting lineup. Casey Sanders and Nick Horvath were given the task of playing with a newfound energy while *only* rebounding and setting screens. Shane,

Dunleavy, Chris, Nate, and I were to think of each game moving forward as if we had a loaded gun, and by game's end, we were not to leave any bullets in the chamber. Our mentality from that point on was to let it fly.

Our game plan was mastered during those four days of practice in preparation for North Carolina. The matchup on March 4 against the Tar Heels would be for a share of the ACC regular-season title. Watching sports commentators on ESPN in the days leading up to that game did nothing but motivate our team. Everyone, including the Blue Devil–loving Dick Vitale, had the Tar Heels winning in a landslide.

When we stepped onto the floor of the Dean Dome, we knew exactly what the strategy was. We were going to run every possession, regardless of a make or miss, turning the game into a track meet. The only question was who would get tired first. North Carolina went big that night with Kris Lang and Brendan Haywood, at 6'11" and 7'0", respectively, and it played right into our hands. A couple of minutes into the first half, during a break in action, I glanced over at Haywood, who had his hands on his knees and was breathing like he'd just gotten done with a one-hour workout.

We got this game, I remember thinking to myself.

By the middle of the first half, the Tar Heels went small and tried to play our style of ball, but it was too late. Battier, Dunleavy, Duhon, and I combined for 89 of our team's 95 points that evening. I had 33 points against a team I couldn't wait to dominate. We wanted it more that evening and realized that Coach K was right: with this new style, we were going to win a championship.

I was averaging around 29 points a game and shooting 51 percent from the field in the early rounds of the 2001 NCAA tournament. When we got to the Sweet Sixteen, I was pitted against UCLA's Earl Watson. Watson was a tough-nosed kid out of Kansas City who was willing to do anything defensively, short of a felony, to take someone out of their game. He confiscated all of your personal space. Scratching. Clawing. Holding. Arm-checking. Tripping. Pulling your shorts down on the court. That's just a partial list of Earl's bag of tricks. During the game, he kept jawing at me, letting me know I was his "bitch"—to be exact. It was just what I needed.

Thank you, Earl, and have a safe trip back to Westwood.

After we handed them a 76–63 loss, a reporter brought it to my attention that I had gone on a 19-point run. Not fully paying attention to him, I replied with a typical Duke PC response about how our team had the firepower to go off in spurts like that.

"No, no, no," he said, "I mean that *you* went on a run and scored 19 straight yourself."

I did what?

After doing away with USC a round later, it was off to the Metrodome, in Minneapolis, for the Final Four. I absolutely hated playing there. Depth perception is everything for a shooter, and nothing messes with that more than stadiums seating 60,000. The dome had a huge gap between the backboard and the crowd, and I struggled to gauge the distance between me and the basket the whole time.

Early in our Final Four game against Maryland, I remember Shane and Chris involved in a ball screen on the right side of the court, with Dun-Dun at the top of the key and me behind the three-point line on the left side. Maryland didn't trap the ball screen, which left Chris, with the ball in his hand, turning to attack the middle of the paint. As he drove, Dunleavy's man left him at the top of the key to stop Chris's penetration, so Chris instinctively kicked it out to him. My defender then decided to leave me to guard Dunleavy, who had an open look. Without hesitation, Dun-Dun rotated the ball to me.

I caught it and turned to the basket. There was nobody near me, and I was thinking, *This three is going in for sure.* When I got to the peak of my jump and was just about to release the ball, I suddenly realized I had no idea where the rim was. The entire basket was lost in a sea of fans seated 40 feet behind the rim. I had no choice but to blindly fire away, and I remember the ball hitting somewhere on the glass, like something out of a dodgeball game. Everyone looked at me like *Jesus, dude, what the hell was that?* I was just thankful it hit a piece of the backboard.

I missed eight of my nine three-pointers in that game, but the one I did hit gave us our first lead of the game, with about seven minutes to play, after having come back from a 39–17 deficit. We wound up winning by 11. It was Boozer's first game back and there was zero rust: he dropped 19 on the Terps in just 25 minutes of action. I had 23, while Shane had 25 in an amazing all-around performance. I'm still shocked that we found a way to beat Maryland three times that year. (We also knocked them out of the ACC tournament.) They were a fantastic team and ended up winning the national title the following season. But something was special about the year 2001. Beating them in the Final Four set up the championship game against the Arizona Wildcats, the only team ranked ahead of us in the preseason polls.

Unfortunately, I played even worse in the biggest game of my life, but our team played well enough to keep us in the lead throughout. This time, we didn't need a miracle—and a good thing, too, since I had totally lost confidence in myself.

Up only five points with less than two minutes to go, we needed to cushion our lead as I brought the ball up the court. I locked eyes with Coach K for instructions, at which point he grabbed his shirt with his right hand, tugging it down.

He was signaling for "L.A."

I couldn't believe he was calling a play for me after the kind of game I'd had. I looked at him quizzically, and he tugged even harder. If he was putting his faith in me, then who was I to question him?

As Shane set the screen, his defender, Richard Jefferson, chose to completely ignore me as I stood a foot behind the arc. I didn't blame him, since I had shot 1-of-9 from downtown up to that point. But for some strange reason, I saw the basket clearer than I had all night long.

Nothing but net.

Our lead was extended to eight, and we never looked back.

As the final seconds were ticking away, I frantically started jumping up and down with pure exhilaration. Chris was bouncing the ball and screaming my name. I looked over at him, unsure of what he wanted me to do, but he kept waving me over until I finally obeyed. When he handed me the basketball, I was baffled. Without saying a word, Chris pointed toward the ceiling with his right thumb. He remembered that dream I'd talked about at the start of the season, and he made it come true. I threw the ball into the air as the clock ran down to zero, and it felt even better than I imagined.

We were national champions.

7

Decision

•

fter the game, the floodgates opened. My voice mail was full and my e-mail was overflowing with messages—not with congratulations, but from strangers reaching out, trying to land me as a client. Throughout the year, there were agents, financial advisers, accountants, and all sorts of people reaching out, hoping to work with me in the future. But now things had taken on a life of their own. Around that time, I was named first-team All-American and the National Association of Basketball Coaches' Player of the Year. I also broke the school's single-season points record. Most people, including those closest to me, assumed my college days had come to an end.

My ultimate goal had always been to play in the NBA. Every other day that season, I'd check online to see where I was projected to go in the draft. It's fair to say it eventually bordered on obsessive. Almost all of the websites had me going first overall.

I'd pay particularly close attention to the projections after a bad game—I had nowhere to go but down, and no margin for error. Had it not been for Coach K's innate ability to keep me from being inside my own head, there's no way I would've ended up playing as well as I did that season. On the court, my focus remained on the team and not on my individual performance.

Off the court was a different story.

With my sophomore season in the books and the championship in hand, my parents were having conversations every week with different agents. The 2001 NBA draft was two months away and I was still slated to be the No. 1 pick. Personally, I knew what I wanted to do.

When we returned to Durham with the national championship trophy, our school held a celebration in Cameron Indoor. Coach K addressed the crowd, then Shane, and as he was wrapping up, the fans began to chant my name.

"JASON WILLIAMS! JASON WILLIAMS! JASON WILLIAMS!"

As I stepped up to the podium, I had no idea what I was going to say, so I went with generic praises and thank yous. As I was winding down, the crowd interrupted me with a loud chant.

"ONE MORE YEAR! ONE MORE YEAR! ONE MORE YEAR!"

Always looking for others' approval, I said exactly what they wanted to hear. "I can't wait to do this again next year." The crowd erupted.

I came off the podium thinking to myself, *What the hell did I just do?* I sat on that stage wondering how I would be able to wiggle out of the commitment I'd just made. I began to panic about what would happen if I went back on my word. The love and support from Duke Nation meant everything to me. Would they ever forgive me if I went with my gut and declared for the draft?

A few days later, I sat down with my parents and went over the pros and cons of leaving.

PROS LIST

1. Money. An absurd amount. $17,286,153 over four years, to be exact, if I was selected first overall.
2. I would finally have the financial freedom to do what I wanted, whenever I wanted.
3. Competition. Kobe, Iverson, Marbury, Jason Kidd, and all the other stars I had dreamed of playing with and against.
4. Jordan factor. Washington had the first pick, and there were rumors that M.J. was planning on leaving their front office to play that season.
5. Travel. Flying private in Gulfstreams, staying in five-star hotels, renting yachts.
6. Business. Tapping into the Duke connections K had always been talking about. Finally being able to take care of my parents.
7. Lifestyle. Specifically . . . the women. I was with Noelle at the time, but I wasn't exactly a saint. The combo of money and fame would drastically change things in that department.
8. Leadership. Shane was leaving, and it was going to be my team.
9. Injury. What would happen to my draft stock and earning potential if I stayed another year and got hurt?

CONS LIST

1. Maturity. Physically, I was ready. Mentally? No shot.
2. Family. My parents would look to manage "the family business," which was another way of saying they'd be managing *me*.

3. Money. It can do as much harm as it can good.
4. Friends. Who would I be able to trust? How many "friends" would come out of the woodwork looking for a handout?
5. Distractions. Women and fame would for sure get the best of me.
6. Education. I had promised my parents I would get a degree.
7. Coach K. Losing what would be another invaluable season under his wing.

In my mind, whichever side won out, it didn't even matter to me. I was playing the role of the good son, appeasing my parents at every turn. Rightfully so, they were adamant about me weighing all my options, which included the inevitable sit-down with my head coach.

Sitting in the common area of K's office—this one at least three times the size of his former—we spoke about a number of things: where we thought my development as a player was at the time, things I needed to improve upon (i.e., my abysmal free-throw shooting), maturity and leadership skills. We talked about how different the team culture would be, going from a winning program ripe with tradition to a losing NBA franchise. We broke down all the options, as if we were drawing up a play. Except this wasn't a game. This was my life.

He said, "Jason, I want you to take all this information and process it. Once you leave this room, I want you to truly think about what it means to be different. I don't want you to follow the norm. I want you to blaze your own path. I want you to be a pioneer."

I always looked to my parents and Coach K for guidance, and all three encouraged me to make this momentous decision on my own. It was a given that my parents would feel let down if I chose to leave without first getting my degree. Education meant every-thing to them. And K truly wanted what was best for each and every one of us. He loved me like a son. My staying another year would surely have given him a better chance of winning another national title, but even so, I am certain that my best interest was his only agenda. His call was that I would stand to benefit from another year learning how to lead. And he was right.

But I still should've left.

And he should've told me to go.

I know Coach K would've supported whatever decision I made, but it was a very different time then. Players didn't nor-mally leave him as underclassmen. But when you're projected to be drafted in the lottery, let alone the No. 1 pick overall, you *have* to go. Time has proven this to be the case. Today, even Duke is not immune to players leaving early in this one-and-done era. Luol Deng, Kyrie Irving, Austin Rivers, Jabari Parker, Jahlil Okafor, Justise Winslow, and Tyus Jones are all "guilty." The present-day Coach K is different—for the better—than the 2001 Coach K. Back then, he wasn't as willing to adapt to the ever-changing landscape of college basketball the way he has so successfully done today. And he has two more national-title tro-phies to show for it.

Financially, it's almost always going to be in the player's best interests to start his pro career as early as possible. The cap on a player's first contract essentially makes it a paid internship—a well-paid one at that—and the sooner it expires, the sooner the really big money kicks in. Pro life is always going to be an ad-justment no matter when you begin it—whether you forgo your sophomore year or stay for all four. The adjustment is jarring for young men of all ages.

Overcome with guilt and the desire to get a college degree, I decided to stay for my junior year. We figured out how I would be able to compile enough credits to graduate in just three years— by spending the next summer taking courses. I would need to take three more summer semesters, which was a small price to pay for having a degree from Duke University for the rest of my life.

There would be pressure. Anything less than another national championship would seem like a disappointment. The season before, we went the entire year without falling below fourth in the polls. We ended up finishing the regular season 26–4, stomped the Tar Heels in the ACC final, and went on to win all six of our NCAA tournament games by ten or more points on our way to a title.

We were the preseason No. 1 in the polls, and I was expected to be national player of the year again. We had a strong team returning, which definitely played a part in my decision to stay. Chris and I were back for more, with freshman combo guard Daniel Ewing coming off the bench; Dunleavy and Dahntay Jones, who had transferred from Rutgers, were our forwards; and Booz, Casey Sanders, and Nick Horvath were back at center.

As much as I respected and loved Coach K, there were times when I was angry with him because I didn't understand his thinking. During games, his intensity knew no bounds, and whenever he yelled that my best wasn't good enough, it took every ounce of me not to respond to him with what was really on my mind. I knew better than to shoot my mouth off, but I had to do something to release the frustration and prevent my head from exploding, so I took it out on my opponents. The more Coach K got in my face to challenge me, the more I would try to kill the guy who guarded me on the court.

Looking back, I get it: K pushed my buttons because he knew I played better when I was angry. I don't know when he figured that out—maybe from watching me in high school or from observing how I responded to his various motivational efforts during my freshman year. Who knows? What I do know is we won a national championship, and I became a two-time national player of the year.

I needed anger. And Coach K almost always did a masterful job of pushing me to the edge without going too far.

Almost.

It's no accident that Coach uses military metaphors when he talks about a team; attending West Point and coaching there had a huge influence on his life. He would often say to us, "Either you're in the trenches with me and we're going to fight, or if you're not willing to fight, I want to make room for people who want to be in the hole with me." I've watched him extend his arm to somebody and say, "Do you need help getting in the trenches with me? Let me pull you in. Here's a branch, here's your end— grab it." And if you don't grab it, "Okay, well, I'm going to put my hand out for somebody who wants to grab my hand and who wants to be in here with me." I've seen people get lost in the mix because they didn't want to buy in completely, or they didn't find a way to express themselves to the point that he knew they were fighting *with* him instead of against him.

But one time in my junior year, he went too far. Or so I thought.

We were in Charlottesville facing Virginia late in the season. Our record was 25–2 going into that game. We were near the end, and despite my atrocious performance, K designed a play for me to drive the ball to the basket.

My stat line at that point was: *4-for-13 from the field, 1-for-7 from downtown, 8 turnovers, 6 assists.*

We had been here before, where K would put his faith in me late in games regardless of how I was playing, but *this* wasn't the right call in my book. Booz had 33 points and had missed only one shot, while Dunleavy really started to heat up at the end. So when the time came for me to run the play he designed, I ignored his call and deferred to someone else. We ended up losing the game by three points.

I will never forget that walk back to the locker room. It was brutal enough to have fallen short, but knowing that the onus was square on my shoulders after deliberately disobeying our coach was intolerable.

UVA had these tight, confined spaces for the visitors' locker room. I was sitting next to Chris, who was even more distraught than I was. The loss clinched the ACC championship for Maryland, but I knew we could bounce back and still win the NCAAs.

I put my arm around Chris, trying to take responsibility for my actions. Trying to be a leader.

"It's my fault," I told him. "I messed up, not you. I was dog shit."

That was when I heard Coach K chime in.

"Get your arm off of him. You're not thinking about him. You're not thinking about us. All you're thinking about is the draft and leaving. You're not committed to this team. I can't believe you would do that. The play was designed for you and you didn't care. You just did whatever you wanted to do."

I was having my very own Chris Carrawell moment. I'd defied our coach just like he had two seasons earlier. And to make matters worse, I handled the situation immaturely.

"This is a bunch of shit!" I yelled as I got up from my seat.

"You're always on my case!" I then took a few steps in his direction while punching my fist into the palm of my other hand. "You're always on me about leaving for the NBA. If I wanted to leave Duke, I would have left last year!"

I caught myself then and there, frozen in my tracks, as I saw the look of disappointment in his eyes. Not knowing what else to say, I started to backpedal and make my way back to my seat. I could only imagine what everyone else was thinking after witnessing my outburst.

"Never have I ever, *ever* had a player talk to me the way you just did. Ever. I'm so disappointed in you."

After that night, there was a little distance between Coach K and me. He didn't say anything directly to me about the incident, but for the next couple of practices he put me on the blue team. Starters were on the white team. That was all he needed to say. Once again, I was angry, so I channeled that rage to punish whoever tried to guard me. It didn't matter that I was on the blue team; we were winning every scrimmage. I had challenged Coach K and it was the wrong thing to do, but I benefited in the end. It was yet another valuable lesson in a long process of figuring out who I wanted to be.

I'll never forget what legendary UCLA coach John Wooden said to me on the day I received the John R. Wooden Award as collegiate player of the year in 2002. We were talking about what it takes for a player to succeed. He said that there are two types of players in this world. The first kind runs directly into a wall and says, as he lies on his back, "Woe is me; I can't believe I ran into the wall." The second player runs into the wall, falls down, gets back up, runs into the wall again, falls down, gets back up, and keeps doing that until he breaks through the wall. Then he says, "I knew that wall never defined me." Coach K's job was to guide us through to the other side of that wall. Every time we fell down, he was there to send us running right back into it.

My last game in a Duke uniform was in Rupp Arena, in Lexington, Kentucky, against Indiana in the Sweet Sixteen. During the second half, we were up by 17 points, but we hit a dry spell offensively and Indiana crept all the way back. Before I knew what had happened, we were down four with 11.1 seconds left after A.J. Moye hit a pair of free throws. Coach K wanted us to push the ball upcourt and immediately call a time-out. Instead, our inexperienced freshman Daniel Ewing received the inbounds pass, pushed it up the right-hand side of the floor, and let fly with an ill-advised three-pointer. The ball hit the back of the rim and bounced directly to me near the top of the key. My first instinct was to shoot the ball, but, being a junior now, the game had slowed down for me immensely and I knew that a rushed shot wasn't a good shot. I took two steps back to get behind the three-point line and fired, making sure I leaned into my defender as I elevated, hoping and praying to draw a foul. Sure enough, Dane Fife collided with me once I released the shot. As I'm lying on my back, the next two sounds I hear are the whistle and the net.

Delirium.

I was going to the line with a chance to tie the game with 4.2 seconds to go.

This was the kind of moment I had always dreamed of. I thought of the countless times in the backyard of my house when I'd dribble the basketball, counting down out loud, "*Five, four, three,* and Williams drives and takes a shot . . . *two, one* . . . and the ball goes in and he wins the game for his team!" Just like hundreds of thousands of other kids have done.

But here it was for real.

As we went to the bench for the time-out, Coach K brought out his clipboard and said, "When Jason makes the free throw, we're going directly into 41 defense." He gave me no other option but to hit the shot. He didn't give us any scenario for what we would do if I missed. As usual, he only focused on the positive.

When we came out of the time-out, I felt like I was alone on the court. I couldn't see or hear anyone. Just before I stepped to the line, Chris looked me in the eyes and said, "We're going to win this game. Make the free throw and the rest will take care of itself."

I stepped up to the line and the referee passed me the ball. I proceeded with my usual routine, thinking of nothing else but the ball going through the net. I aligned my right toe with a nail that is always in the center of the free-throw line. I positioned my left foot so it was shoulder width from and six or seven inches behind my right foot. Like I'd done thousands of times before, I spun the ball, staring at the rim, and took three dribbles.

One. Two. Three.

As I was on my third dribble, I took a deep exhale and let it fly. The shot felt better than any other shot I'd taken in my life.

Good . . . Wait, not good!

The ball rattled in and popped out. Booz got the rebound off the right block and we had the win in our hands, but he brought the ball down, allowing Jared Jeffries to swipe at his put-back attempt.

Game over. Season over. Duke career over.

On a damn free throw.

8

Bulls

●

met with a bunch of different prospective agents once I declared for the 2002 NBA draft. Duke set up all the meetings. Only guys that were "Duke approved"—super power brokers like David Falk, Arn Tellem, Lon Babby, and others who'd represented all the greats over the years. I remember all these impressive presentations, and then when it was Falk's turn, he came in with nothing except the story of how he made Michael Jordan into a global icon. That was enough for me. Sold!

But David Williams wasn't having it.

"That's great, David, but how are you going to help *my* son?"

And Falk had a solid response, laying out his customized plan for my future, but it was a lost cause. The process was over before it even began—my parents already knew who they wanted for me. After we won it all my sophomore year and it looked likely that I'd leave, my mom and dad had sat with an agent named Bill Duffy from the Bay Area and taken a liking to him right off the bat.

Duffy was in store for a very exciting draft. He already had Yao Ming, who was 21 years old at the time, and would soon land the Kansas Jayhawks' star power forward Drew Gooden. And now he had me. The way things shook out, Duffy's three new clients were taken in the top five of the draft.

I'm not sure who decided to officially change my name from Jason to Jay, but I know it wasn't me. A couple of weeks before the draft, we were in my hotel room in midtown Manhattan, preparing me for media hits later that day. Right before we were about to leave, we saw a news report about the pending trial of the Nets' Jayson Williams in connection with the death of his limo driver. He ended up getting a five-year prison sentence, and I recall at the time thinking, *Damn, he had it all and threw it away.*

Right then and there in the lobby of Trump Tower on Fifth Avenue, Duffy and his team suggested how it might be a good idea to distance myself from Jayson, while also distinguishing myself from Sacramento's Jason "White Chocolate" Williams, who had made a big name for himself compiling one highlight reel after another throughout his career.

My mom vehemently disagreed and started going on a rant about the importance of my given name. Frustrated by the back-and-forth debate, I finally chimed in.

"You know what? I'm just excited to get drafted. You guys decide. We can figure it out later."

The next day I woke up, opened the newspaper, and learned that I had been rechristened. Right there in the sports section was an item about my changing my name from Jason to Jay. I still think it would've been nice to have known what my new name was before the rest of the country did. It marked a turning point after which my life no longer felt like my own.

The evening of the draft was surreal. My mom, my dad, Noelle, my boy Graham, and Bill Duffy sat at a round table, just feet away from the stage in the Theater at Madison Square Garden. I wore a black tuxedo with a white shirt and pale silver tie. I thought I looked great. The pictures today tell a different story. I can't help but shake my head when I look at them now. The jacket had shoulder pads that didn't sit right at all; the shirt-tie combo made me look like a waiter; the pants were too baggy. As bad as mine was, Drew Gooden's outfit was exponentially worse.

Very late the night before, Duffy had popped by my hotel room to let me know Chicago was a lock at No. 2. Houston would be taking Yao. He added that Golden State was working the phones with Chicago to do a swap to move up one spot so they could take me. I was appreciative to have the information in real time, given that this was where the next chapter of my life would unfold. So while it was definitely anticlimactic when Commissioner David Stern called out my name as the second pick in the draft, it took nothing away from the moment.

I got up, showed love to everyone at my table, and headed for the stage to begin my life as a pro. All I kept thinking about as I made my way up the stairs was *Please don't embarrass yourself on national TV by stumbling on the way up.* I would have never heard the end of it.

Concentrate. Don't you dare trip, Williams.

It was all business once I arrived to greet Commissioner Stern.

"Congratulations, Jay," he said, shaking my hand while patting me on the elbow as we posed for the camera.

"Thank you, sir," I replied.

In the midst of all the flashes and cheering, I realized that all of the attention focused on me was now based on what people hoped I would do, not on what I had done. I, Jay—not Jason—Williams looked over at my parents and knew they were no longer just my caretakers but now also my business partners. I had an accountant, a lawyer, and financial advisers. I was a fledgling brand built on a product I hadn't yet produced.

My parents and the financial firm I started working with had organized my draft party for later that night at a club called Metronome, which was one of the hottest spots in the city at the time. They hired a part-time private security guard named Tim Marks to shadow my every move. Tim's a light-skinned African American man who probably stood around 6'7" and must've weighed over 250 pounds, all muscle. I knew in advance that we'd hired him, but I had no idea what it was going to entail. It was like I was handcuffed to Tim the whole evening, at a private gathering with just our friends and family. It was ridiculous and made me so uneasy the whole night.

With Noelle by my side—and Tim—I made the rounds to thank everyone for coming out. Things were going really well, and I was enjoying myself. That is, until I heard a familiar voice from behind me trying to get my attention.

"Jason! Jason! . . . Hey, *you*!"

I prayed it wasn't who I thought it was, but then I heard her say, "Jason . . . it's Jenny!"

Jenny was my ex-girlfriend from my freshman year of college. We dated for a while until my wandering eyes got the better of me. Trying to be cool with the situation, I turned around to face her and quickly introduced her to Noelle. After a brief exchange, I asked how she had heard about the party.

"Oh, your mom invited me," she said with a proud smile on her face. Noelle had the opposite look on hers.

I then continued to walk the room, holding Noelle's hand, with her a pace behind me, when all of a sudden I felt someone tug on my shirt.

"Hey, hon. I am so, so proud of you," she said while kissing me on the cheek. It was Lauren. Lauren and I had been something of an on-again, off-again item during my sophomore year of high school. She was a gorgeous girl of Puerto Rican descent, and if possible, she looked even better that night than how I remembered her from when we were 16. Before I even got a chance to ask, she expressed how happy she was that my mom had invited her.

My mom and I are extremely close, so it wasn't unusual for her to meet the girls I dated, but inviting them to my draft party when she knew Noelle would be by my side? That was some cold-blooded shit. And it only got worse from there when, maybe five or ten minutes later, I noticed *at least* two other girls I had been involved with in the past. So not only did my mom use her own Rolodex to track down the women of my past, she even enlisted my friends to gather up any girl I had been with. My once anticipated draft party had turned into a night of putting out fires and cleaning up vomit. Noelle drank herself into a stupor, as anyone probably would've in her situation, and threw up all over the living room of our suite when we got back.

I was still hot the next day when I ran into my mom in the lobby. "Why the hell would you do that?" It was almost a rhetorical question, as I knew the conversation would go nowhere.

She replied how she "just" wanted everyone who loved me to be there, like she was doing it out of the goodness of her heart. *Bullshit*, I thought to myself as I rolled my eyes and walked away. The battle between Noelle and my mom had begun in earnest.

The whole night wasn't exactly a disaster. One amazing memory from the party that I'll cherish forever was when I hung out with an unexpected guest. I didn't know then that one day I would grow to revere this man. Just like my childhood friend Dre, my boy Graham was a UNC fanatic, and he recognized someone outside trying to get into the club. Graham was drunk, looking for a lady—any lady—when he took it upon himself to get the guy inside. After freeing myself from Noelle, who was a complete mess, and shaking Tim off me for the first and only time that night, I felt Graham drape his arm around my shoulder with fun-loving, drunken aggression. He was double-fisting two bottles of Dom Pérignon when he handed one over to me. We clinked bottles and both took a long swig. When my head tilted back down, I saw a third bottle on its way in for yet another cele-bratory clink, paired with a voice that was unmistakable.

"You're the only Dukie I mess with, man. Congrats!" It was Stuart Scott, the one voice that for me was synonymous with ESPN. I was in complete shock as the three of us chugged our bottles at the same time. I despised most media members back then. They were the enemy—always looking to kick you while you're down. But Scott was different and I was thrilled to have him at my party, kicking back, drinking, and bobbing his head to the same music as us.

Hungover as can be and still furious with my mom, my par-ents and I left that next morning for Chicago. My annoyance, though, began to morph into gratitude as the plane descended into O'Hare. We were all in first class and would have a limo driver waiting for us at baggage claim. It was one of the first times it really sank in that because of me, my parents were going to get everything they'd ever wanted. They were so happy and proud.

We headed directly to the practice facility, where I saw my fellow draftees and new teammates Roger Mason and Lonny Baxter. All three of us hailed from the ACC and had competed against one another for years. Mason would go on to enjoy a ten-year NBA career and now serves as director of player relations for the NBA Players Association. Sad to say, things didn't go as swimmingly for Lonny. He was one of the nicest guys around but fell on some hard times after flaming out as a pro. His lowest point—I hope—came on August 2006 when he was arrested just a few blocks from the White House after firing a .40-caliber Glock handgun into the air.

So there we were, sitting on a stage in the Berto Center and being introduced to the media. I was in the city that Michael Jordan built, and the questions from the press reflected the hopes and expectations that a brilliant new Bulls era was about to begin.

At Duke, the constant emphasis was on the team. Halfway through the press conference, I saw that that was not the way things were going to be here: I was the No. 2 pick in the draft, so I was supposed to be the franchise's savior.

The Bulls had been a disaster ever since Jordan left in 1998. Their combined .223 winning percentage since then averaged out to around 18 wins per season, and I was their fifth lottery pick in the past four years. Chicago fans were restless and wanted us to start winning yesterday; they'd gone through four dire seasons mostly under Tim Floyd and Bill Cartwright, who was entering his rookie season as a head coach. Cartwright had apparently earned his shot after serving five years as an assistant coach for the franchise. I guess their thinking was that his ties to the front half of the Bulls dynasty would help bring the team back to its winning ways. They also wanted someone who had played the center position to mentor our teenage lottery picks as they were going into their second season. Eddy Curry and Tyson Chandler were both very gifted, but at opposite ends of the court: Tyson had the potential to become a defensive great, while Eddy possessed the offensive skill set to be an unstoppable force.

I knew right away that Jamal Crawford was the best player on the team. Cleveland had selected him with the eighth pick two years prior, and the Bulls made a wise choice in trading Chris Mihm for his rights on draft night. From day one, the Bulls' coaching staff established that we would not play together. We would have to battle daily for the starting spot. This move created colossal discord right out of the gate. We were copacetic off the court, but wanted to kill each other on it. The media didn't help matters by stirring the pot on a daily basis about who should play over the other. And why, you ask, wouldn't they pair us up in the backcourt when Jamal was a 6'6" shooting guard and yours truly was a 6'2" point guard? Your guess is as good as mine.

A year filled with some ups and mostly downs really began when I got my first look at Jalen Rose, who'd been traded from Indiana to Chicago seven months earlier. Jalen walked into the locker room on the first day like the mayor—big smiles, loud talk, high fives all around—and I thought, *This dude can't be serious.* It was like a door-to-door salesman going about his business while hating every last minute of it. Jalen was shipped out of Indiana unwillingly because he was at odds with his then head coach, Isiah Thomas. And this was after his general manager, Donnie

Walsh, promised him he wouldn't be traded. So I wasn't buying the bullshit he was selling, but nevertheless I was thrilled to have my favorite member of the Fab Five on the team. I'd heard that veterans tend to play themselves into shape, but I had no idea what that meant until he got undressed.

It was just like that scene in *The Great White Hype* when Damon Wayans's character, James Roper, takes off his robe at the heavyweight championship weigh-in with a massive gut after training on doughnuts and cigarettes. I didn't hear a damn thing Jalen said after his shirt came off; his mouth was moving, but I just kept staring at his midsection like *Damn, dude, are you serious?* The funny thing is, he wasn't even a little ashamed to be so out of shape. Instead, he cracked jokes about his conditioning.

We'd run up and down the court once or twice, and Jalen would score and then have to come out for a breather. He'd go back in again, score, and a minute later come out for another rest, hunched over on the sideline like he was about to have a heart attack. After catching his wind, he'd go back in and hit a couple more buckets. No one could stop him, gut and all. It was like watching the eighth wonder of the world. He didn't care what anybody else thought, which was the polar opposite of my 21-year-old self. And that's the beauty of who Jalen was, and still is, to this day.

It didn't take long to realize that Jalen's physical condition was the least of our team's issues. The Bulls had won six championships running the complex triangle offense, and had hired Cartwright to teach it to us. We were lovingly referred to as the "Baby Bulls." And here we were, one of the youngest rosters in the league, being instructed to learn the most convoluted offensive scheme in basketball.

The triangle is a read-and-react system that has an endless sequence of options, with each new pass keying the next set of choices. The only teams that had ever been successful with it were the Bulls with Michael Jordan and the Lakers with Kobe Bryant, two of the greatest players ever; the guards who thrived in the system alongside them were spot-up shooters like B.J. Armstrong, John Paxson, and Steve Kerr.

Our guards, however, weren't perimeter players—we liked to run free, use a ton of ball screens in the open court, and play fast. Being a half-court team overthinking each and every pass was the last thing our team needed.

We were in the Boston Garden for my first professional basketball game. I scored 13 points and had seven assists and seven rebounds, but I missed all five of my free throws, including four in the last 90 seconds. Afterwards, Jalen told the media, "He has to step up and make them. In the NBA, we just call that choking."

I would call that choking in college basketball, too.

He added, "You don't take it easy on rookies, especially ones who miss free throws in the fourth quarter."

I was definitely not used to teammates calling me out to the media, and couldn't believe he'd go to those lengths after a win, and my first pro game no less. It was the last thing I needed as I was just beginning to cope with the adjustment from college ball to the NBA, not to mention an offensive scheme I was struggling to understand. I remember waking up the next morning and seeing the comments he made in one of the papers, thinking to myself, *Fuck this dude.* I didn't speak to him in practice, or anywhere for that matter, until our next game, a day later, when we were forced to interact on the court.

It only took two games into my pro career to find out that my leash was much shorter than ever before. One or two mistakes on the court and I'd find myself out of the game. At Duke, I was encouraged to work through my screw-ups; in Chicago, any error landed me on the bench. I watched Jamal go through it, too. I played 33 minutes against the Celtics in my first game ever and played only 20 in the following game against the Hornets.

After winning our first two games, we lost 13 of the next 15. That was as many losses as I had had my *entire* three years at Duke. Twenty-one months of college basketball and I had just accumulated as many losses in just over four weeks in the NBA. If I were to find any solace during that stretch, it would have to be from my seventh game of the year.

We were home against Jason Kidd and the Nets. Jamal was scratched that night, back in his hometown of Seattle on personal leave after his grandmother had fallen ill. I find it funny that the one game I didn't have to worry about being yanked off the floor for a mistake ended up being the best damn game of my career. Bill was "forced" to let me play through, and as a result I started to find my groove. The ball was in my hands more, I was involved more, and the next thing you know I'm making great passes and getting defensive rebounds. I'm playing like my old self again, and I'm doing it against one of the all-time greats. At 6'4", 215 lbs, with a motor that never stopped, Jason Kidd was the most electrifying point guard I ever played against. The more he pushed, the more I pushed, and we both ended up with triple doubles that game. I was the first Bull to get a triple double since M.J. For one night, at least, I was the player everyone had hoped I would be. And . . . we *won*.

My stat line: *26 points, 14 rebounds, 13 assists in 45 minutes of action.*

In the locker room, Jalen handed me the game ball and said, "This is yours, man. You deserve it tonight." Bill barely said anything to me, which I found to be bizarre, but I remember thinking, *Whatever. Move on.*

I dropped 20 points on Milwaukee in the following game with the extra playing time, but after Jamal returned, we ate into each other's minutes once again.

In the middle of our first West Coast swing, we were playing the Lakers on a Friday night. I was mentally drained from getting our asses handed to us night in and night out, so I decided to take a taxi to the Staples Center in the afternoon before the mandatory call time for the game that evening. I wanted to go in early and shoot hundreds and hundreds of jumpers for at least an hour—until it felt right.

As I walked onto the floor, I saw one other player, already in a deep sweat, going through his moves at game speed. I just watched him for a minute before I snapped myself out of it and got to work. After a little over an hour, I was spent. And I still heard the ball bouncing at the other end. He was still at it. I sat down in the first seat I could find, just watching this guy in disbelief. I thought to myself, *There's no way his legs are going to be fresh for tonight.*

Twenty-one points, ten rebounds, seven assists, and five steals later, Kobe Bryant proved me wrong.

ON A BAD team, players are always checking their statistics. And the selfishness that follows from that can affect everything that happens on the court. We were all guilty of trying to sabotage one another. After it happened a bunch of times to me, I'd had enough, and decided to take part in the charade. I wasn't going to be the only one to have his stats take a hit. So if I had the ball with four seconds or less to shoot, I'd defer to someone else, forcing them to heave up a contested, low-percentage shot instead of it falling on my shoulders. If that teammate wound up with the ball in his hands with no time left on the shot clock, then *he'd* be charged with a turnover. Neither scenario looked good on the stat sheet, and I got away clean. It was a good old-fashioned game of "hot potato."

And I developed a masterful countermove for when a teammate tried to sabotage me: I'd just let the pass go out of bounds, transferring the turnover back to the passer.

Coldhearted? Sure. But it's a coldhearted business.

ON THE DAY after New Year's, the Greatest of All Time had returned to the United Center for just the second time since leaving the Bulls in '98. Michael Jordan was about six weeks away from turning 40 and he was back in uniform. Things weren't going much better for the Wizards that season, however, as they had already accumulated 17 losses in just 31 games. The announcement of his name during the team introductions received a standing ovation from the Chicago home crowd for what must've been at least five minutes. It was as if he'd reawakened his audience from the glory years.

It was exhilarating to have the opportunity for our playing careers to overlap. I was determined to shut him down that night. I'd convinced myself that I needed to win our crowd back, and I used that as motivation to get as hyped up as possible. Even though it was Jalen who had the defensive responsibility of checking him, I ended up guarding him a few times on switches. One possession, while he was backing me down on the left wing, as I jammed my right elbow into his hip, trying to steer him toward the baseline, I started jawing at him.

"He ain't doing shit," I said. "He ain't scoring on me."

Even though I was a rookie, and just 6'2", I felt like I was stronger than most guards in the league. I weighed 205 pounds and had really good position on Jordan that particular play.

Or so I thought.

He just looked at me as he kept backing me down and then blurted out, "Here it comes, over the right shoulder."

All net.

As we inbounded the ball, I thought, *That did* not *just happen.* I'd like to believe Coach K would've given me a pass for allowing the previous play . . . and the next . . . and the one after that, too. This was the first time I'd ever met one of my childhood idols, and he was cussing me out and calling me every name in the book. I may have been one of his easiest "victims" as I played one of my worst games of the year. M.J. wasn't himself either that night, so he decided to take it out on the next team just two days later, dropping 41 points with 12 rebounds on the Pacers.

The next month, I was in Atlanta for the All-Star Game. I wasn't an All-Star, but I was a part of the festivities that weekend as I played in the Rookie Challenge. It's since been renamed the Rising Stars Challenge, where the best of the rookie class play the best of the second-year players. One of my best friends since AAU days, Scooter Braun—or Scott, as I call him—was the biggest nightclub promoter in Atlanta. Scooter, a senior at Emory at the time, personified what it meant to be a hustler. Before the days of social media, he linked up every college in a 30-mile radius and provided them with access to the hottest nightspots in the area. Atlanta was the hotbed for hip-hop back then. It didn't take Scott long to figure out how the music industry was wired there as he leveraged his nightlife connections to get a major leg up in the business. Many of the local heavy hitters were fascinated with how he was able to get white kids to flock to these historically black clubs.

So the night before the Rookie Challenge, Scott threw an epic party that I attended with my girl Noelle, my boy Dre, and of course . . . my "shadow," Tim Marks. All of six months removed from college and here I am sitting in the back of a limousine, on my way to *the* party, when Noelle points out a massive billboard for an Adidas campaign with my image on it. One minute my face is on a schedule magnet put out by the Duke Athletic Department, and the next I'm on a billboard in Atlanta. I was now a star, and I hadn't even done anything yet.

When we pulled up, there must've been hundreds of people in line trying to get into the club. It was chaos. Tim got out of the limo, rallied a few other huge security guys, and parted the crowd like the Red Sea. I felt like a real celebrity as we made our way inside. We entered the most star-studded VIP room I had ever been in. Within minutes, I'm in a drinking contest with Shaquille O'Neal while he's seriously arguing with then heavyweight champion of the world Lennox Lewis about which one of them would win in a fight. Next thing I know, I'm in a deep conversation with Ashton Kutcher as his girlfriend Brittany Murphy and Noelle are sitting in the corner becoming fast friends.

Many shots later, Scooter and I found ourselves in the main club having a dance-off against Justin Timberlake, Ashton, and his boy from *That 70's Show*, Danny Masterson. Noelle and her new best friend Brittany were watching us battle it out when all of a sudden someone shoved Brittany. Ashton sprung into action, and that was when all hell broke loose. The next thing I know, I'm being picked up three feet off the ground like a ragdoll by

Tim. He carried me all the way to the other side of the club as if there was an assassination attempt on my life. Instead of rushing to my girl's side to make sure she was okay, Tim made me his girl. Flat-out embarrassing.

The party may not have turned into the success Scooter was hoping for, but things worked out just fine for him. Today he owns two record labels, including one he formed with Usher, and he represents Justin Bieber, Ariana Grande, and other huge acts.

IT'S DIFFICULT TO describe the impact money can have when you're so young and impressionable. Long gone were the days filled with anxiety about how we'd make ends meet. Bills in the mail were treated with the same concern as PennySavers and catalogs. I put my parents on the payroll and picked up three new homes within a matter of months. My biweekly paycheck was unfathomable.

$163,113.43.

I lived on Chicago's "Magnificent Mile," one of the best-known shopping destinations in the country. So naturally, I'd find myself tempted into making extravagant purchases. I bought my mom a Cartier diamond necklace for thirty-five grand and a $15,000 fur coat. I picked up a $5,000 Cartier watch for my dad. I treated myself to a pair of platinum dog tags for twenty, a platinum Rolex President Day-Date for forty, a couple of Andy Warhol prints for thirty.

My teammates and I gambled all the time. Shot for shot in shootarounds before games, hell, even rock-paper-scissors sometimes! On the flights, we'd drink beer and shoot craps in the aisle. There'd be cash all over the floor and in everyone's grasp as they'd ready their bets, just hundreds of dead presidents staring back at us. Like so many others on the team and in the league, I'd pack my Louis Vuitton backpack full of cash for the trip, and if I forgot to load it up beforehand, I'd play on credit. Credit came in handy when games escalated quickly with the dice not rolling your way. One time we were on our way to Cleveland from Chicago, and before we even got over Indianapolis, I found myself fifty grand in the hole to Jamal Crawford. Duration of the flight? Forty-nine minutes.

I'd always look forward to my shooting games with Eddy Curry. The funny thing is, he'd be the one pushing them more than I did. Eddy used to bet me $1,000 per three-pointer, $5,000 per step-back jumper, $2,500 per baby jump hook. Bets were always random. And when we'd call it a day, whichever of us owed the other would fork it over in the locker room before heading to the showers.

As disorienting as this new life had become, I tried my best to remain grounded. Those closest to me lived in the real world—the same one I had come from just months earlier. The more money I made, the worse I felt about others going through their struggle. I began to realize how even the smallest of gestures could have a major impact on someone.

On long road trips, our athletic trainer, Fred Tedeschi, would give us an envelope with a per diem of a grand or more. I always kept it sealed for when I got back home. I'd hand the envelope to a bunch of kids who were always playing drums outside my building during the freezing winter months. Being a millionaire at 21 was a gift.

The season we were having, however, was a curse.

It wasn't just the fact that we were losing; it was how—to Boston 91–69, to Dallas 114–87, to New Orleans 105–87. We lost to Sacramento by 13, to Utah by 20. Even when we did lose games in college, it was typically by no more than two or three points. I had to make a major adjustment going from a winning environment where accountability was everything to watching teammates take a game or two off because their finger hurt. We'd be on the bench down by 25 and players would lean back, call a ball boy over, and tell him to chase down the digits of random women in the stands.

Guys smoked weed constantly. And I did, too, from time to time, but never before games. During a time-out once, a teammate nudged me in a joking way, asking me if I smelled popcorn. I looked back at him, seeing his eyes all bloodshot and glossy, thinking to myself, *Are you fucking high right now?* The truth is, I knew he was high, because I'd smoked with him during our days off. I'd smoked weed with a bunch of guys that season, including Corie Blount, who six years later ended up serving time in prison for trafficking over 29 pounds of marijuana.

The promise of bonding together as a team was replaced with an every-man-for-himself mentality. We were completely dysfunctional. The lowest point came late in January when I rolled my ankle in Miami. I went against everything I believed in as a player and decided to sit out instead of playing through the pain. I put myself on the injured reserve list for a couple of weeks and missed five games.

Plain and simple: I quit.

I had never quit anything before. I was a fighter. I was as defeated as I'd ever felt in my life. I wasn't particularly close with any of my teammates, the press was all over me, and I could only imagine what the fans were saying, what the guys upstairs were saying. Earlier in the season, I'd made ill-advised comments to the press about how the city of Chicago deserved better and perhaps the team needed to be shaken up if things didn't right themselves. At the time, I thought my being outspoken would display leadership, but being a rookie, it completely backfired on me. And today I completely understand how foolish I was for not keeping quiet and letting others do the talking. I was too young, immature, and inexperienced. And my numbers didn't exactly help matters. I'd have a very solid outing followed by two or three duds in a row. I was in no position to lead.

I ended up no better than anyone else by season's end, but rather a part of the problem. I started to rationalize doing selfish things like hopping on a private plane to Vegas fresh off a practice with a game the next night. Or being cocky about playing well in a double-digit loss at Orlando and rewarding myself by partying with friends that same night in Miami. And what happened the next day against the Heat? I'd play 30 minutes and shoot 1-for-10 from the field and 1-for-4 from the line. I remember Coach Bill Cartwright pulling me aside to discuss my questionable commitment to the team after he heard from teammates that they'd seen me out late the night before. Then, all I could think was how messed up it was that they sold me out, and why wasn't their commitment being called into question if they were out late partying, too? Now, I just shake my head thinking about how idiotic I was for not holding myself to a higher standard.

One of the very few bright spots that year was our assistant coach Pete Myers, who was competitive as hell but had a funny way of calling us out. Eddy Curry, who was just not catching on to the triangle offense we played, kept setting the wrong screens, and each time he did, you could hear Pete slapping his legs and stomping his feet on the sideline. He took his displeasure to the next level: Eddy came up and set the wrong screen—again—and Pete yelled, "God dammit!" Next thing you know, Pete's asking, to the tune of Michael Jackson's "Smooth Criminal," "Eddy, are you okay? Are you okay? Are you okay, Eddyyyy?" It was the funniest shit I had heard in my life. We were in the middle of a game and Pete was playing the dozens. "Eddy, can you hear me? Can you hear me? Can you hear me, Eddyyy?" Crazy comedy.

Eddy wasn't the only one to feel Pete's comedic wrath. We were playing Milwaukee once, and I couldn't stop Sam Cassell for any amount of money. The guy was as slow as molasses, but he just kept getting bucket after bucket. He finished with 29 points and nine rebounds after going 14-of-16 from the free-throw line. Weeks later, when we were watching tape of that game as we prepared to face them again, Pete stopped the tape, looked at me, and said, "J Will, what's up? Sam just busted your ass about nine possessions straight. When are you going to get some pride and play some defense?" Then he started the tape and yelled, "It's about to be *ten* possessions. Watch this. Watch how he does this one on you. Watch now. God *damn*, boy, that's embarrassing. I don't even want to invite my family to games if you're going to play defense like that."

Early on, I hoped I'd eventually learn to respect Bill as a coach, but as the season progressed, my opinion of him didn't change. As far as most of us were concerned, he was in way over his head.

The first red flag came just four games into the season when we were in Toronto. During a time-out near the end of the game, Bill was drawing up a complicated play when Jalen reached over and tapped at the clipboard, saying, "We're not runnin' that." I thought, *Oh, this should be good. Coach is about to lay into his ass.*

Bill just stared blankly at Jalen, then looked at the team and proceeded to tap the clipboard.

"Okay, Jalen, what do you want to run?"

"Give me the ball," he demanded.

I just sat there on the bench thinking, *Did he just tell the coach
what we were going to do? And did the coach just bitch out?*

It'd be one thing for a coach to take suggestions. It's another
altogether to flat-out cower to a player's demands. Luckily, Jalen
ended up making the shot to take us to overtime. Otherwise, I
wouldn't have been the only one to recollect that day. I just noted
it and moved on. But then there was a litany of other issues that
arose during the season. It almost felt like a constant chatter of
complaints from the guys, including me, about Bill not knowing
what he was doing.

This might've only been Bill's second year as a head coach, but
he had been an assistant on the Bulls bench for five seasons before
Jerry Krause chose to promote him to the head job. He got fired
fourteen games into the next season. After close to a decade as
an assistant coach for the Nets and the Suns, Bill left to coach in
Japan, and today he's coaching the Mexican national team.

During the final seven games of the season, I really felt like I'd
finally found my mojo. We decided to shift into a three-guard
set where Jalen, Jamal, and I shared the floor together for long
stretches of time. For once, it didn't feel like we were stagnant,
with the ball dying in one player's hands. I developed a terrific
chemistry with Jamal, and both of us ended up playing our best
personal basketball during that stretch. We stopped battling with
each other and started working together. It started to become *fun*
again. I shot better than 60 percent from the field over that span,

and my legs felt stronger than ever. Jamal, meanwhile, was on a tear, averaging 23 points and six assists per game while shooting almost 50 percent from the field. I had never played with someone as talented as Jamal. His speed, his handle, his nose for the basket—he had everything. And he's still doing it—at an even higher level—all these years later. Our final game of the season was in the United Center against reigning MVP Allen Iverson and his 76ers on April 15, 2003. If that night was a harbinger of things to come, then things were looking up. Yes, Iverson ended up with 42 points, but we still won the game by nine. Jalen, Jamal, and I combined for 67 points on 22-of-42 from the field, 22 assists, 9-for-9 from the free-throw line, and 10-for-15 from downtown that night. And to top it off, Eddy went 14-of-16 from the field for 31 points. There was much to look forward to heading into the following season.

A few minutes into the third quarter, Jamal got the ball, drove hard to the rim, took a hit by Eric Snow, and fell to the floor. I sprinted over to my teammate for maybe the first time all year and went to pick him up. By the time I got over to Jamal, Jalen was already by his side, extending his hand. I reached out to grab Jamal's other hand. Here we were, helping to pick each other up after months of breaking each other down. We were becoming a team. Finally.

Things were going to be okay.

9

Rehab

•

've obsessed over how my life could've ended up differently had
I swerved just a foot more to the right and missed that pole al‐
together. But then I think about what would've been had I not
swerved at all.

Gone.

I was still here, ravaged by one serious setback after another.

June 19, 2003

I severed my left leg's femoral artery, the main artery that pro‐
vides oxygenated blood to the tissues of the leg, and required
a vein graft. The sacrum, the triangular bone at the base of my
spine, was cracked and needed a large metal pin, which I have to
this day because I refuse to have yet another surgery to remove it.
My pubic symphysis, the cartilage connecting my right and left
pubic bones, pried apart about ten inches, causing severe nerve

damage and a virtual coin toss on whether I'd be impotent the rest of my life. The dislocation of my knee not only tore every ligament in the joint but also severed my peroneal nerve, which provides the signal from your brain to lift up your foot. Losing this nerve meant I would never properly control my foot again.

During the first couple of weeks in the ICU in Chicago, the doctors focused on closing the severed artery in my left leg so I wouldn't lose it or, worse, my life. They then operated on my pelvis to close the gap in my pubic symphysis and the crack in my sacrum. It wouldn't be until after I got to North Carolina that I would undergo surgery to repair the leg and my peroneal nerve.

July 2, 2003

I met my surgeon, Dr. Claude Moorman, once I arrived at Duke University Hospital. Dr. Moorman, a behemoth of a man who comes from a long line of football players, continues to oversee the Duke Sports Medicine Center today. As physically imposing as he was, he was the dictionary definition of a gentle giant. Upon my arrival, he immediately brought me into surgery to wash out all of my wounds and close my fasciectomy incisions in order to keep any of my lacerations from getting infected after the long trip by land and air.

While recovering from the procedure, my doctors began to ponder the next steps. Four days later, Dr. Moorman, Dr. James Andrews, who has operated on one Hall of Famer after another, and Dr. Richard Steadman, another top orthopedic surgeon based in Colorado, held a conference call to brainstorm the best way to reconstruct my knee. It was like having a dream team of surgeons come together to formulate the game plan.

July 25, 2003

Thirty-six days after my accident was when the surgery to repair my knee finally took place. When people think of a joint dislocation, they might picture a finger or a shoulder, where treatment involves popping it back into place. But with a knee dislocation, the bones of the leg completely separate (the femur is separated from the tibia and the fibula) and the ligaments that hold the bones together tear. Without proper and timely treatment, there is a risk of losing the leg altogether. The surgery the doctors performed on my knee involved reconstructing my anterior cruciate ligament and reattaching my posterior cruciate ligament. My lateral collateral and medial collateral ligaments also had to be reconstructed. They had to reattach my biceps tendons and also had to do a peroneal nerve graft.

Translation: I was in very bad shape.

By this point, I had been on my back for more than a month, unable to conjure the strength to move. My entire left leg was elevated and restrained for a month after the procedure. The amount of scar tissue and stiffness that built up during the healing process was staggering, and in turn, the challenges that lay ahead when it came time for physical therapy were astronomical.

By mid-August—five operations later—it was time to begin the rehabilitation process. My next location following my stay in Duke University Hospital was five miles away at 4643 Owls Wood Lane. It was a beautiful 7,400-square-foot home that sat on six acres, which my parents rented for us in a pinch. They wanted me to be close to the Duke medical facilities, but it just so happened that I was all of two houses away from Coach K. I was going to need his strength, and this made it easy for him to stop by to provide it. In addition to my parents living with me, my mother's friend Laurie stayed over from time to time to chip in. And then there was Deuce, Buddha, and Duke, our three rottweilers. And let's not forget my day-to-day nurse, Judy, who helped me get through the worst of it.

A day or so later, once I'd settled in, my physical therapist, Bob Bruzga, and my occupational therapist, Jill Freck, started coming over for preliminary sessions. We began with tasks as simple as testing my sensations. They would touch my leg with a metal pointer at different points going up and down, asking me if I could feel it or not. At first, I could feel practically no contact whatsoever. They tried applying different amounts of pressure to see at what point my body would respond.

It barely registered anything but pain.

And the pain was two things: constant and unbearable. It was so bad that it would often wake me up from a dead sleep. As a result, I needed someone to sleep in my room those first several weeks to help me shift positions, go to the bathroom, get water, and pat my face down with a compress after I'd wake up in a cold sweat from reliving the accident in my dreams.

Everybody would pitch in, changing out my bandages, checking on the swelling, and making sure the stiches were still intact. I had never felt more like a charity case. My left foot was held in a 90-degree position with a metal plate pressed up against the bottom of it to maintain the integrity. A large metal apparatus we dubbed the Titanic enclosed my entire left leg, leaving just a sliver open for ventilation from my toes all the way to my hip. Whatever part of my leg wasn't enclosed by this contraption was fully covered in bandages.

I was, for lack of a better word, stuck.

For the first few months I could only sleep on my back, but as my strength began to return, the doctors said it was okay for me to change positions. Being able to change sleeping positions is one of those little blessings you don't notice until you can no longer do it. I wasn't strong enough to turn myself; my core was too weak, and I had the Titanic pressing down on me.

Between the physical and psychic misery that was my current state, I resorted to numbing myself from having to face this head-on. I no longer wanted to have to think about defecating on myself in bed and having to ask someone else, not named Judy, to not only clean up my feces but also to wipe my own ass afterwards. It was just too much for me to handle.

This was the start of my eventual addiction to OxyContin.

I had hit rock bottom, convinced that I no longer wanted to live.

Two months and five days following the accident, I stood up out of bed for the first time . . . for three seconds. It took four people to get me there: my mom, my dad, Laurie, and Judy. I swung myself to the side of the bed. My dad lifted me around my torso while my mom and Laurie held me under each arm. Judy had to hold my leg straight out because it was still in the brace. As I got halfway to standing, it felt like my pelvis was going to snap, so they sat me back down right away. We tried again a little later, after the pain subsided. I was finally able to raise myself to a point where I was standing straight up with my leg extended outward. Standing gave me the same sensation I felt when I got hurt—like scalding hot water was being poured from my pelvis down to my foot. The pain was so excruciating that I sat down yelling in agony shortly before passing out. While I hadn't lasted long on my feet, the act itself was a major victory. It was amazing to think that my life would now be measured in such small firsts.

September 4, 2003

It took my family two and a half hours to get me from my bed to the car. I left the house for the first time to go to physical therapy, where they were going to take my leg out of the brace.

Sitting on the therapy table at what was once called the Finch-Yeager Building at Duke, with Bob to my right and my parents and Noelle to my left, I looked at my left leg and couldn't believe my eyes. My leg was like a wire. To give you a sense of how small it was, the blue brace I had to wear around my thigh doesn't even fit around my forearm today. Just the sight of my leg was nauseating.

When Bob said to me, "Pull your foot up," I pulled with every single ounce of strength I had. To stare at my foot while in a dead sweat just from trying to move it, only to watch it go nowhere—not even an inch—broke me mentally. It was as if I had no leg and somebody had surgically attached a rope to my pelvis and hung a weight shaped like my foot from it.

After I collected myself emotionally, I was ready to continue with the session. Bob held my leg ever so gently with both of his hands and tested my flexibility. Sitting at the edge of the table, with one of his hands supporting the back of my left thigh just above the knee and the other holding my calf, he slowly began to bend my leg to check its dexterity. My leg bent only 45 degrees at best, and the process was grueling. By the time he finished bending my knee, it felt like my heel was touching my ass.

I had a long way to go.

On top of everything else, I suffered from phantom pains due to the nerve-regeneration process. My leg could've been on fire and I wouldn't have felt a thing. But I absolutely felt every bit of the nerve trying to regenerate itself—it was as if someone were stabbing me in every part of my leg with a dull knife blade. Doctors compared the pains to childbirth. The nerve was projected to heal itself about an inch per month.

I had over a foot and a half to go.

For every small step forward, I couldn't help but feel that I was taking two giant steps back. My knee refused to go any further than 50 degrees, and all the efforts from physical therapy were to no avail. Arthroscopic surgery was suggested.

October 25, 2003

It was always comforting to see Dr. Moorman; however, I was hoping it would be for checkups and consultations rather than another dreaded surgery. While the orthopedic scope on my knee wasn't nearly as invasive as my other procedures, it still required me to go under the knife. Here, Moorman inserted the arthroscope—a slim, pencil-like instrument with a camera at the end—into my knee joint, which fed an image to a monitor. On the screen, he was able to see the structure of my knee down to the most minute detail. That allowed him to remove any of the damaged scar tissue.

The next day, it was right back to rehab.

It was imperative that I get the knee joint moving right away so no scar tissue would build back up. Inflammation became a major issue, which hindered my flexibility post-op. Every day was monotonous—my knee would get stretched harder and harder, only to gain no more than a couple of degrees. The only variation was whether it was Bob or Jill going through the motions with me. My doctors, not settling for that outcome, decided a more aggressive surgery was necessary.

My patience had worn out by this point. We already knew what surgeries I would have to get, but now it was one disheartening surprise procedure after procedure.

November 19, 2003

Now, this one really sucked.

My doctors determined that I would need a knee manipulation. The procedure was done under anesthesia to prevent my body from naturally resisting. With me unconscious, the doctors would be able to systematically, and progressively, bend the joint to tear it apart. It requires a massive amount of physical force—you can actually hear the scar tissue pop—and the joint quickly becomes more flexible.

When I woke up from the procedure, my leg was clamped to a contraption called a CPM (continuous passive motion) machine. It would help reduce the chances of further scarring. For the week following the surgery, my knee was constantly being mechanically bent and straightened. After that, the goal of therapy became to maintain the range of motion that had been recovered during the procedure. Then there was the challenge of managing the pain that stemmed from the inflammatory trauma. It was understandable to everyone why I was taking two OxyContins per day and some Oxycodeine for short bursts of relief.

By mid-December, I could bend my knee to 95 degrees. It was progress. But one afternoon I felt a pain I had never felt before in my knee. I quickly developed a fever over 100 degrees and was taken to the ER, where they discovered I had a staph infection that had created a hole the size of a silver dollar on the outside of my left kneecap. Doctors had to perform a scope to treat the infection. I was quarantined for a short stint. When I awoke after the procedure, I had a PICC line in my arm—a catheter for IV antibiotics that remained in my arm for five or six weeks. My physical therapy had to come to a halt to give my body time to recover once again. During those several weeks on an antibiotic drip, I lost about 10 degrees of range of motion in my knee.

Our bodies are wired to resist—what medical experts call "muscular guarding." I would need a specialized form of therapy. Jason Gauvin was the answer. Jason was in his mid-thirties at the time and had transferred to Duke from Stanford right around the time I arrived in Durham. He was an outstanding physical therapist, and an even better human being. I recall him confiding in me how the process was very difficult for him at times, since he essentially had to cause his patients great pain in order for their overall condition to improve.

It wasn't until February that I continued with my physical therapy out in the open. Up until then, I was really not in any condition to be rehabbing around others. But the real reason for staying behind closed doors was to keep the media at bay. After my parents talked me into leaving the house for the first time back in mid-September, I had shut that experiment down, outside of a few Duke-related events and such. My mom and dad and others in my inner circle thought it would be a morale boost for me to get back into the world.

So there I was in a wheelchair on Frank Bassett Drive, with Chris Duhon guiding me through throngs of Duke football fans as we made our way into Wallace Wade Stadium. There wasn't enough Oxy in the world to get me through that day. And I tried.

It was the most humiliating experience of my life.

People were yelling out words of encouragement, some were crying, while others were whispering just loud enough as I passed by about how I had thrown it all away. Many came over to say how I was in their prayers and touched my leg, which was outstretched at a 45-degree angle. And that part really added insult to injury. It's hard enough to blend in when you're in a wheelchair, but even trickier when you need at least four feet of clearance in front of you at all times because one of your legs is sticking straight out. One good Samaritan after the next yelled for people to clear a path so the "cripple" could get by. I once walked among these people with my head held high, proud to be me. Now I would've done anything to have been just another face in the crowd.

Group therapy in the beginning sucked. It was a constant reminder of how long the road to recovery was going to be. I couldn't help but look around the training floor, seeing people from all walks of life working their way back to full strength, in much better physical shape than me. Last summer, I was preoccupied with catching up to Kobe Bryant's conditioning, and now I'm comparing myself to some 63-year-old in a wheelchair working away on an arm cycle.

I had been out of the wheelchair and on crutches for close to five months when Jason decided it was time to take both of them away.

"Stand."

"Stand?"

"Yes, Jason, stand."

"I am standing."

"No, stand with equal weight on each foot."

I still had the brace attached to my left leg, so I didn't have control of my foot. I remember my foot just dangling as I softly placed it on the ground for the first time, trying to shift my weight over to the left side of my body. I screamed as a sharp jolt of pain shot through my back to my knee and all the way down to my foot. I was certain all eyes were on me after I had brought this unwanted attention on myself, but it was probably all in my head. The truth is, everyone was fixated on themselves, striving to get better. After popping an Oxy to manage the sudden throbbing pain, I spent the next hour trying to put weight on that side while Jason stood behind me, his forearms under my armpits to hold me. He would rock me from side to side, and I would lean a little left as I squeezed my eyes shut, cringing in agony. Then he would quickly shift all of my weight back to my right side. After ten or so tries, I was drenched in sweat, completely spent. It took months for me to get to the point where I was able to stand on my own two feet again.

It was at some point during March Madness that Jason began to reteach me how to walk. I had absolutely no idea how I was going to move at all with my left leg trapped inside a bulky metal thigh-to-calf brace, one that must've weighed close to ten pounds. Much of the density from it was because of my ankle-foot orthosis, or AFO, a brace that was attached to my calf to keep the ankle stabilized. The metal plate under my left foot, which kept it flexed, also contributed to much of its weight.

As Jason walked me over to the parallel bars, my mind was racing with trepidation. All the hard work it had taken to get to this point, and now, after eight months, I was finally getting ready to take my first steps.

When I got to the parallel bars, I hesitated at first before parting with my crutches. I wanted this more than anything, but I wasn't sure if I was ready. I couldn't handle another setback. With Jason standing at the other end, I firmly gripped the bars, with my head down, staring at the floor. I counted the steps it would take to get to him. I don't remember how many, exactly, but I do know it left me in considerable doubt.

Jason reminded me that this was what we'd been working toward so hard these past several months, and that I wasn't a person to back away from a challenge.

But he was wrong.

I wasn't that person anymore. I was broken. It wasn't just walking I had to teach myself all over again. I needed to recapture the fighter in me. I just stood there without saying a word, hands squeezing the bars so tightly I could see the white in my knuckles. I became even angrier as I continued to question myself. The vexation quickly morphed into sorrow and pity. I was just standing idle, a shell of my former self. I started to cry.

Jason came over and put his arm around me, saying that everything would be okay and that I had nothing to be afraid of. He reminded me about one of my goals, and how much I'd looked forward to showing my son how to round first base one day. But in order for that to happen, this would literally have to be the first step.

"You can do this, Jason. I believe in you."

In tears, I leaned all of my weight over to my right side and extended my left leg. I placed it softly on the ground while still keeping all of my weight on my back foot. Once my left foot was firmly planted, I took a deep breath and exhaled, preparing myself for the worst. Using my arms to hold myself up, I then took the chance. *No pain . . . no pain*, I pleaded with myself, and sure enough, when I shifted all of my weight onto my left leg to take a step with my right foot, it didn't hurt.

It was sore. But there was no pain.

I smiled through more tears, this time from joy, not fear. It was a milestone, for sure, but Jason, almost reminiscent of Coach K, wasn't interested in celebrating until the task was finished.

"Keep coming. Let's go, now."

I made it all the way to the other side to receive my hug. I was physically drained, but emotionally recharged.

It was now time to learn how to balance myself without any assistance—no crutches, nobody holding me up, just me. I had to retrain my body how to find its equilibrium. A year earlier, I was rock solid in a defensive stance, trying to stop Michael Jordan. Now I had completely lost the ability to lift my left toes up in the air. This malady is called drop foot or foot drop. Either term is acceptable, but neither one is preferred! I couldn't stabilize my left ankle, which is imperative for balancing. Unable to pick up my big toe—something I still cannot do today—I was prone to falling over. Jason and I tried time after time, and at best, I was able to hold my balance only for a few seconds. Jason started to hold a stopwatch during our sessions to see how long I could stand on one leg. We practiced every day for weeks on end—until one day he came up with an idea that was a game changer.

Basketball had always been a positive force in my life, and Jason decided this was as good a time as ever. He grabbed a basketball and tossed it my way. I caught it and looked up at him in confusion. Before I could even ask, he said that he wanted me to continue to balance myself on my left leg and *just* focus on catching the ball with both hands while throwing it back to him as quickly as I could. *"Go!"*

When the ball hit my hands, I felt like my former self. My athletic instincts took over. I was no longer worried about being unable to pull up my big toe or stabilize my ankle. My attention was squarely on the ball. I got lost in the game of passing the ball back and forth, at peace, for once, to be out of my own head. Then all of sudden, Jason caught the ball and didn't throw it back.

"Hold it!"

I brought my right foot down a few seconds later and took a deep breath. Jason stopped the clock, walked over, and showed me.

24 seconds.

A much-needed breakthrough.

I was on my way.

My knee's range of motion was around 110 degrees toward the end of May, but I had started to have some serious pain on the outside of the joint. After going in to the Duke hospital for an MRI, it was determined that I had a small meniscus tear. A fifth surgery was needed.

May 7, 2004

Doctors performed a meniscus repair on my left knee and also provided me with the *gift* of one final manipulation to get me back to full range of motion. I had been hovering at the same mark for nearly three months, and this was the last attempt to get me to the finish line.

While I was recovering, the therapist told me that the swimming pool at the sports-medicine facility would quickly become my new best friend. To help me regain strength, the pool provided a less weight-bearing environment in which to do my walking and balancing exercises. A grown man in a pool with braces and full-body floaties was not the sexiest look, but my vanity would have to take a backseat. Each day, I was challenged to do as many laps as possible, with the hope that I would surpass the total from the day before.

I'll never forget one day in the pool when I was watching a woman doing laps. She had to have been at least 75 years old, wearing a black one-piece, a white swim cap, and goggles as she moved maybe a mile per hour. My athletic instinct to compete kicked in. I entered the pool thinking to myself how I was going to crush this woman. *Take her down, Jay. She ain't shit.*

My newly adopted rival was just passing me as I lowered myself into the water, and I was determined to catch up. At first I was making good headway, but I still found myself behind after the first two laps.

Then it was over.

My breathing got heavier by the second, and my eyes started to burn from the chlorine. Excuses. As she gradually started to pull away, I thought to myself, *Pick it up, Williams. You pick this shit up right now.*

Trying to kick it into a higher gear, I watched helplessly as she made her first attempt to lap me. Just as I could feel her presence, she unnecessarily yelled out to caution me.

"ON YOUR LEFT! PASSING ON YOUR LEFT."

We were the only two people in the pool.

"Old Lady Goggles" lapped me at least ten more times that session, then said to me on her way out, "It's okay. I remember my first time in the pool after my surgeries."

I was exhausted as I smiled back at her, trying not to say anything rude in response but thinking, *Dammit, woman, I've been in the pool for months.*

July 9, 2004

It had been over a year since the accident when I had my third electromyography (EMG) procedure. The doctor inserted a three-inch needle deep into my leg muscles while I was hooked up to electrodes that would read the response of the muscle to the stimulation of the nerve. It sent a series of electric shocks up and down my leg while the doctor moved the needle around for added measure—not once, but 15 to 20 times. Being surrounded on the court by taller guards and huge big men, I'd always felt undersized, even at 6'2". But when the doctor was testing every inch, my leg felt as long as Manute Bol's.

The third time was not the charm in my case. The nerve had still not fully healed. It had been over a year of horrendous pain stemming from the nerve-regeneration process, and I still had more to go, with no guarantee of a complete recovery. I was distraught.

The doctors decided we would wait a few more months to see if anything improved. After five more agonizing months, there were still no signs of recovery. The next step was a tendon transfer to relieve my drop foot.

December 7, 2004

I would have my ninth operation in 18 months. This time, the procedure required cutting a tendon located on the inside of my left foot and reattaching it to the top of the foot. I was hoping for a Christmas miracle.

And I got it.

Three months or so following the surgery, I was finally able to pick up my left foot two to three inches off the ground. It was just enough for me to clear my gait while walking without having to hike my hip up. Keeping this coordination going while just walking around was daunting, to say the least. The idea of mastering the process at the pace it takes to be a point guard in the NBA was next to impossible.

LEFT: With Mom, back when I had hair.

Even at two years old, I was the life of the party.

I still look up to my father to this day.

I was proud to be named
the first All–American at
St. Joseph's High School.

ABOVE: With the
"United Nations" on
prom night (*left to right*):
Dresden Baluyot, Brian
"Darkness" Wilson,
Felson Sajonas, and
Peter Stein.

With Mom, Dad,
and Assistant Coach
Mike Thompson on
Senior Night.

Proof that I did pass the ball in college. *(Photo courtesy of Duke University Athletics)*

There's nothing better than dominating the school that I once wanted to attend. *(Photo courtesy of Duke University Athletics)*

Getting emotional before my last game against North Carolina on Senior Night. Oh yeah, I dropped 37 on the Heels.

(Photo courtesy of Duke University Athletics)

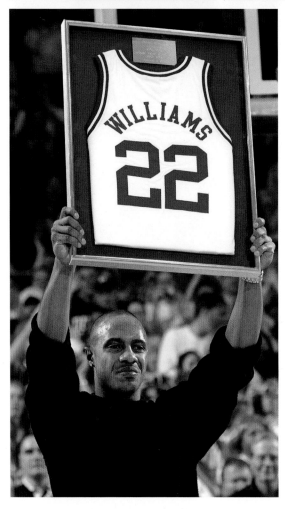

ABOVE LEFT: Coach K and I embracing the 2001 National Championship trophy together.

ABOVE RIGHT: Sharing a moment with the great John Wooden after he presented me with the 2002 Naismith College Player of the Year Award.

Proud to take my place among the Duke legends on the night my jersey was retired. *(Photo courtesy of Duke University Athletics)*

TOP: Being introduced to the Chicago Bulls media for the first time after being drafted number two overall. *Left to right:* General Manager Jerry Krause and fellow draftees Roger Mason and Lonny Baxter. *(Photo courtesy of Bill Smith/Chicago Bulls)*

Above, right, and overleaf: The moments that made me think I had a bright future in the NBA. *(Photos courtesy of Bill Smith/Chicago Bulls)*

(Photo courtesy of Bill Smith/Chicago Bulls)

© 2003 Chicago Tribune. All rights reserved.
Distributed by Tribune Content Agency, LLC)

The motorcycle—
or what's left of it—that
changed everything.

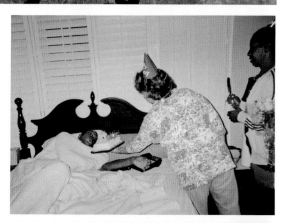

I celebrated my
twenty-second birthday by
not being able to move.

Trying to find some
happiness with my mom's
friend Laurie Adams. Nine
months after my accident, my
leg was still encased in a brace
I called the Titanic.

Being wheeled out of the hospital by my former Duke teammate Chris Duhon during my first public appearance after being laid up in the hospital for two months. *(AP Photo/Bob Jordan)*

Trying to find my way outside of Duke's Cameron Indoor Stadium. *(AP Photo/Bob Jordan)*

On the ESPN set with (*left to right*) Rece Davis and Seth Greenberg. It's not quite the same as being *on* the court, but I'm still connected to the game I love. (*Photo courtesy of Duke University Athletics*)

•

I HAD AN unbelievable team of doctors and therapists who worked with me for countless hours each day. They were as invested in my well-being as I was—sometimes way more—and every one of my victories was a victory for them as well. They listened to my fear and frustration, but instead of letting me wallow in my inadequacy, they reminded me that my recovery required determination. Jason didn't just focus on the physical rehabilitation during our sessions; we talked about how things were *really* going. Our dialogue was focused on who I was, not on what I had done or hoped to do. He was always concerned with what head space I was in.

The challenge for those around me was that I was unable or unwilling to express how much pain I was in psychologically. The more that people close to me wanted to know how I was feeling, the more pressure I felt to spare them my distress. I usually responded with a simple "Just gotta keep fighting" or "I'm taking it one day at a time." All sorts of generic, bullshit lines. I'd quickly change the conversation: "I'm okay—how are *you*?" Here I was, surrounded by people putting their lives on hold for me, waiting for some miracle that might never come. I didn't want to show any mental weakness, and I internalized a lot of my emotions. But Jason seemed to recognize this right away. There was something redemptive about our connection.

I had to trust that my therapists and doctors knew how to help my body heal. I needed to be patient with my body and believe that I would come through to the other side. I am forever grateful to them for pushing me through the pain—emotional and physical. They never let failure be an option.

10

Complications

•

Cheating had become the norm during my short stint in the NBA. If you're a professional athlete on the road and you're not being promiscuous, it's because you're actively trying not to be. Sleeping with my college girlfriend's roommate was one thing, but the league was a different ball game. One of the many ways the life of a pro athlete is seductively warped is seeing how many women want to be with you. The sheer availability of casual sex will test any man's desire to be faithful, and from someone as young and inexperienced as I was, it called for a level of strength and self-denial that I couldn't summon at the time, or didn't want to.

The process wasn't that difficult, because the road map had already been preapproved and laid out. All you had to do as a rookie was piggyback with one of the veterans who knew how the game was played.

The team charter lands in City X at 11:00 P.M. The veteran already knows where to go and who to go with as soon as we touch down. After arriving at the team hotel, the veteran and his crew take off for an evening out. You arrive at the club at 12:30, already attracting attention when you walk in the door because of the crew's abnormal height and authentic platinum and diamond jewelry. Chatter begins and heads turn as security escorts your crew to the VIP area, which is ideally located in a section of the club where women can easily spot you and your buddies. After "tipping" the security guards off with $100 apiece, you now have a blockade of massive men around you not letting anyone penetrate the circle. Five security guards only attract more attention, which is better for your crew in the long run because it makes you look that much more important than you really are. Random guys make attempts at saying hello but are held at bay while you are scoping out the scene, seeing who is deserving of your time. Cocky . . . yeah, I know.

Soon the floodgates open as eight girls arrive at your booth. Ten bottles of Dom follow with sparklers as people stare in awe. If you aren't satisfied with the talent at the table, you tap the security guard on the shoulder and point to someone else you want him to bring over.

The guard walks over to the lady, points you out while telling her that you would like to chat with her and buy her a glass of champagne. She then gathers her friends and everyone comes over to your section. As the music continues and the champagne flows, either a number is going to be exchanged or a move to leave is going to be made. By the time the end of the night rolls around, enough headway has been made that the conversation usually ends up continuing back in your hotel room.

Depending on city ordinances, I would get back to the hotel anywhere from 2 A.M. to 6 A.M., usually tipsy or drunk. The night would lead to casual sex. Sometimes the girls would stay over until the morning, sometimes they wouldn't. I never made any promises to anyone and always justified my actions thinking that I wasn't married yet and was just having fun.

Guys would even arrange nights like this during the actual games. A ball boy would write a note, pass it to a woman and her friends in section such and such, and that night we'd party. Some players had regular hookups and just stayed at the hotel, ordered room service, and called it a night, while other guys loved to go out and "hunt."

Times when I would see players pull up to the team charter before a road trip and kiss their wife and kids goodbye would break me. They'd jump on the plane, spend the next ten days with two or three women, come back home, and greet their family as if nothing ever happened.

And who's to say I wouldn't be doing the same once I had a wife and kids of my own?

With the exception of some brief breakups here and there, Noelle and I were seeing each other pretty much throughout my entire first year in the NBA. She would find text messages on my phone from other girls, hear from random friends that I was messing around with this one or that one, and use other various means to expose my philandering ways. She was no fool. Noelle and I were close to calling it a day at the time of the accident, but I asked Kevin to reach out to her anyway. I didn't even give it a second thought. And within 24 hours of taking his call, she was there. I always wanted her around, but now I needed her more than ever. So when she arrived, her presence brought this tremendous warmth, which helped lift my spirits. Once again, we reunited, and that gave me a piece of happiness to hold on to at a time when I felt like I had lost it all.

One of my favorite days before my accident came late in December of my junior year. I had just dropped 38 on Kentucky at the Meadowlands, but that wasn't why I was on cloud nine that night. After the game, we were officially on Christmas break, so I left from there with Noelle and her parents to go back to their hometown. It was an hour's drive to Freehold, and Noelle and I sat in the back of her dad's car, trying our best to catch up after not seeing each other for the past few months. The long distance was taking its toll on both of us. She had this whole other life playing for the women's basketball team at Wagner University and traveling all the time. And I was completely consumed with my career at Duke and all that was to follow. She knew how much buzz I was getting at the time, but all she cared about was how I was doing—off the court.

Later that night, at a house party thrown by someone she knew, I pulled her outside to the backyard for a conversation. I told her that I loved her and that I wouldn't let anything get between us. I saw myself marrying her one day and I didn't want us to give up. I then said I would do anything she wanted to make this work. She looked at me for a brief moment without saying anything and then told me to:

"Take a hit of my blunt and do 15 jumping jacks."

I did as instructed.

"Now scream as loud as you can how much you love me."

And I did that, too. We just laughed the night away and thought this was the beginning of the rest of our lives together.

•

IT IS STILL safe to say that the tenth of September 2003 marked the most difficult birthday of my life. While I was done associating myself with the number 22 on the court—perhaps forever—it was time to come to grips with what my life had come to at . . . 22 years old. I had envisioned what this year of my life was going to be like on the court, having just started to figure things out, but instead here I was lying in a hospital bed in a rented home in North Carolina, wallowing in my sorrow, wishing to be alone.

Noelle had come down from New York City to be there with my parents, Laurie, and Kevin as we "celebrated my special day." They bought a cake with rich vanilla frosting and 22 candles. Everyone was so cheerful as they walked into my room singing Happy Birthday with the candles lit. I was so high on Oxy that I must've thought it was the Fourth of July. I knew my family was so happy that I was alive to see 22, but at the moment, with 22 individually lit candles staring back at me, all I wanted was to not have survived the crash.

I was so weak that it took me three tries to blow out all the candles. I'd always had such a strong upper body, but now I had the frame of a ten-year-old child. The scene was sobering: my face was emaciated, and my skin was dry and tight against my cheekbones.

My dad had always been a strong man. After kissing me on the head, he grabbed my hand while I stared at him, crying with shame and guilt. "God has a purpose for you, son," he said. "I've thanked Him for keeping you here every day since that day."

His words moved me that night. I hadn't been thankful. It was the first time since my recovery began in Durham that I recognized how much of a martyr I was being. I was truly blessed to have such great people willing to do whatever it took to help me through this dark and twisted journey. Later that night, while sitting in my wheelchair on the porch with everyone, I just couldn't stop staring at Noelle. One minute she was a bartender in midtown Manhattan, and the next she was spending her days and nights with me five states away. Only a special kind of love could explain why someone would drop everything to come to the aid of her helpless 22-year-old boyfriend who couldn't find the strength to do anything except feel sorry for himself.

What am I waiting for? I asked myself.

Later that month, I made the decision that marrying Noelle was what I wanted to do. Not being able to do much on my own, I turned to Laurie for her help and swore her to secrecy. I knew my parents would be livid if I told them I wanted to get married at such a young age, not to mention only three months after my horrific accident.

So Laurie drove me to the Southpoint mall, about 20 minutes away from where I lived. I was on a mission to buy a ring, but just as with the Yamaha R6, I opted out of doing any research in advance of making a purchase. I would know what to get as soon as I saw it. This process was the only thing that kept me upbeat during the hardest of days.

We ended up spotting Fink's Jewelers while Laurie was pushing me about in my wheelchair. And just trying to get into the store should have been a sign to roll the other way. The doorway had a lip that neither Laurie nor I could get the wheelchair over. Multiple employees rushed over, picked up my wheelchair with me in it, and placed me right in front of a display case. Not embarrassing at all.

I quickly became overwhelmed with how many options I saw and was also very ignorant about the details of what I was even looking for. An older saleswoman approached me and seemed to take great joy in the process of helping me figure it out while pulling out ring after ring. Of course, she started with the most expensive ring after a couple of people had recognized me making such an inconspicuous entrance. Although I wasn't sure what I wanted, I quickly declined the ones I didn't want. After I said no to nearly every ring in the store, the woman told us she had one more option in the back. When she returned, I saw her holding a red box with gold trim, and I knew exactly what was inside. It was going to be a Cartier ring, and I hoped I'd really like it. As she opened the box, my eyes grew wide at how beautiful a ring it was.

"Perfect," I whispered to myself while she talked about the craftsmanship, the number of carats, all of those details that meant nothing to me. I could see that ring on Noelle's finger as we grew old together. Without even asking the price, I just said, "I'll take it," and handed the clerk my credit card. I had already prepared myself for a big price tag, telling myself, *This is your soulmate, and who cares if you spend $10,000 on a ring? You have the money. Do it.*

It wasn't until Laurie handed me the receipt to sign that I learned the price was five times what I had thought it would be. I signed the receipt in a matter of seconds and the purchase was made.

Riding back to my house, I started to panic thinking about how I would explain this extravagance to my parents. They received copies of all my bills and had been questioning my spending from the day I got into the league. Not consulting them on a decision as momentous as this one would most definitely leave them homicidal. So I decided not to say a word. I remember convincing myself that it was my call and my call alone to make. I was spending my own money, and this was something I wanted to do for my future wife.

The next time Noelle came down to visit was in early October. In an effort to try and get some fresh air, I suggested that she and I have a picnic at Duke Gardens. Because I hadn't really thought the process through—seems to be a common theme here—Noelle had to literally navigate my wheelchair up hills and through dirt to get to a shady location that was suitable for our feast. I didn't have a perfect scenario in mind, and as she unpacked the bags of food, I impulsively pulled out the ring. I called her name and she turned.

Noelle, I know I haven't been the perfect man, and for that I am sorry, but I want us to start a new chapter. I want us to be real. I need you by my side for the rest of my life. Will you marry me?

I had never seen her smile as brightly as she did then, and I had never felt as good as I did the moment after she said, "Yes."

When we got back to the house, we announced our engagement to my mom and dad. They stayed silent while we talked, then expressed their thoughts. They were baffled about the timing more than anything else. They were certain that now wasn't the time for such a colossal life decision, that I couldn't know what I truly wanted, especially considering that only a month before I had tried to take my own life. I was not in any place to make sound decisions.

My mom pulled me aside about twenty minutes after we entered the house, in tears that were clearly not from joy. "Just stop with all this movement for a while and be still," she begged.

But I couldn't stop.

I've always been a restless person, and I just couldn't let another day pass where all I did was sulk. The next step was moving my fiancée to Durham to live with us under the same roof. When

I announced this to my parents a couple of days after we got engaged, things went from bad to worse. Up till then, they were able to refrain from lashing out, but this update caused a ripple effect. The tides grew stronger and all hell broke loose.

There are two sides to every story. There were things that my parents had seen from Noelle that raised red flags for them. Years later, my mom told me stories of when she would be cleaning the house while Noelle just lay in bed watching movies. Or when she was cooking dinner and Noelle never even offered to help, sitting at the table waiting to be served.

I wasn't hearing any of it at the time. I was convinced that my parents had it out for Noelle. They didn't want our relationship to work and would try anything to sabotage us if given the opportunity. My mind—though it was overtaken by painkillers—was made up, so I decided to hold my ground. Noelle was by my side, and she could do no wrong in my book.

The inevitable domino effect began, and things started to splinter. My dad announced that if Noelle was moving in, he would be moving out.

"When a man brings a woman into his home, it should just be him and her and no one else." It was one thing for him to take care of his son, but he wasn't about to watch over his son's 22-year-old fiancée.

His position infuriated me. How could we not all live together? The house was massive. Everyone would have plenty of personal space. It was bigger than most bed-and-breakfasts.

The power struggle with my dad took a nasty turn. I told him that if he felt he needed to leave, then he had to do what he had to do. Noelle was coming down to live with us, and that was final. However rash I was being with all these sudden changes, I felt justified in my behavior when I realized that it was me who was paying my dad's salary, so I was in control, not him.

My mom knew that Noelle was in no position to take care of me by herself. She even went to the length of speaking to Noelle's parents, begging them to try to change their daughter's mind about moving down south. She pleaded with them, explaining how her husband was going to walk out on us if Noelle moved in. Unfortunately, they weren't going to tell their daughter how to live her life, so their decision—and mine—caused my family to rip at the seams.

My dad choosing to leave was one of the more hurtful things he had ever done. I understood why he was upset, but I thought it was low of him to bail on us instead of working things through. Things already hadn't been perfect between my mom and dad since I was little. And I think once I was able to give my mom some financial freedom, she used it to distance herself from him. During my rookie year, she often stayed at my place in Northbrook, Illinois, while he stayed back in their home in Jersey. My accident almost forced them to come together in my desperate time of need, but now he'd had enough. He felt that, just as he'd forewarned, I had let a woman cause a major distraction.

My mom, too, was forced to choose between her husband and these two immature, star-crossed lovers. She made her decision based on what was in the best interests of her child, but she didn't have to like it. I still had endless hospital visits, more surgeries to follow, pain management, physical and occupational therapy, media obligations, caring for the dogs, the finances, the maintenance of the house . . .

With her marriage now completely up in the air, my mom moved into the guesthouse. She wanted to give Noelle and me a chance to see if we'd step up to the plate and become real adults. I never once thought about how incredible she was during that time to not only put her own life on hold but also allow it to go up in flames as a result of my actions. I can't help but shake my head in disgust today when thinking about how foolish and disrespectful I was being to the two people who cared for me the most.

Noelle tried her best, but as my mom predicted, her best was far from good enough. She was overwhelmed, not just with the list of duties but also with the culture shock that came with moving from the big city to a rural setting. She had been rooming with another friend in a cramped, converted two-bedroom apartment in the heart of Times Square; now she had just moved into a huge house in the middle of the woods. She was used to a nonstop pace, working as a bartender until late at night. Now Noelle was in a completely different world, one that was tailor-made for my mom but alien to her.

Noelle was happy to assume the responsibility of administering my medication, but on some occasions when she didn't do exactly as the doctors had prescribed, my mom got really upset with her. Due to the severe nerve damage to my pelvis, it was mandatory that I take a Viagra once a day for my erectile dysfunction. The purpose here was for the drug to stimulate the nerve by bringing blood flow to the area. It took close to five months before I saw any results.

I was given the blue pill once a day, first thing in the morning. One time, however, Noelle inadvertently gave me a second Viagra along with my afternoon meds. I normally would've known not to take it, but on that day, and most others during this time, I was in a complete fog. I was oblivious to the double dosage, and had it not given me hives, I wouldn't have even noticed. Infuriated by the mishap, my mom gave Noelle a sturdy talking to.

Tensions increased between the two of them with each passing mistake or misjudgment, but my mom refused to move out until I was able to walk on crutches, drive myself to town, and manage my pain better. I knew how lonely my mom was, living by herself in the guesthouse with her dog, Duke, and having to walk on eggshells around us, fearing that she was going to explode at any moment. It was as if I could hear the sound of her teeth biting her tongue. She had no one to turn to, and deep down, I felt so damn guilty.

It wasn't until early June 2004, almost a year later, that my mom finally returned to New Jersey to be with my dad. In many ways, her going back to him was a positive sign that my overall health was progressing; however, the tension among the three of us was still very much palpable. My mom and I still spoke every day to put her mind at ease, but our relationship morphed into something very different. It became stiff and regimented for a while. Gone was the playful banter and lighthearted dialogue, until years later.

To add to all the complications, my relationship with Noelle started to be put to the test. All of those uncomfortable conversations about infidelity that were tabled while I was fighting for my life had begun to surface.

And they were not good.

Noelle and I would go back and forth about life in the NBA, and that only resurrected her deepest insecurities from that year. We'd had a tumultuous relationship at times during my rookie season, deciding to call it quits more times than I'd like to remember. She could trust me when I was lying in my bed, unable to move without her assistance, but could she trust me on the road in a hotel room if I was ever fortunate enough to get back in the league? Given our history, I could understand her uncertainty, but I was a changed man. Instead of just hearing her vent, I listened to her and was able to understand where she was coming from. The love between us was as strong as ever, but the trust was fractured.

NOELLE AND I bought our first—and only—home together on September 22, 2004. It was a really beautiful three-bedroom traditional with white brick, tucked away at the end of a cul-de-sac in Croasdaile Farm, Durham. We both fell in love with the place the moment we walked in the door. I remember us being so happy and excited about our future, picturing all the great memories we would make living there.

All we had to do now was make the purchase.

I made the down payment for the home and the vacant lot next door for added privacy. Our realtor happened to be one of Noelle's friends, and my accountant set us up with a mortgage through SunTrust Bank. When it came time to issue the deed to the property, Noelle insisted on having her name included with mine. As much as I loved her, I was very apprehensive about acquiescing. First, our relationship was often pretty volatile, and as much as I wanted things to work out for the long haul, I had my concerns. Second, I still had my parents in the back of my mind telling me to be careful. Were her intentions genuine?

In keeping with the theme of our relationship, I believed I was ready to give in and make peace with the decision. That is, until her mom suddenly inserted herself into the process. This was the same person who, a year earlier, had refused to get involved when my mom begged her to speak with her daughter about postponing the move down south. My guard was officially *up*.

And so the day came when I asked Noelle to sign a prenuptial agreement before we tied the knot. She was adamantly against the idea. She spoke of how her parents had worked together to fight injustices that befell them during hard times, and how far they'd come as a couple because of it. She didn't want to dishonor them by entering into a marriage with a precursor for potential failure. Her reasoning was sound, but my accountant was unmoved. The more I pushed for her signature, the more I pushed her away.

And so began a song and dance that would last for close to two years.

She gave me the ring back and left for New Jersey. I refused to ship her stuff to her unless she agreed to come back and talk. When she arrived, I put the ring back on her finger and told her I didn't care anymore about a prenup as long we stayed together. She agreed to stay and we were happy . . . again. But at some point, we both got cold feet and took some space from each other.

After all I had been through, all that I'd put my parents through, and now what I had put Noelle through by asking her to marry me in the first place, I *had* to make our relationship work. I had no more room in my life for failure and disappointment. I would talk to my mom regularly, asking her for guidance, as I knew it would be from the purest of places.

"Marriage is hard, Jay . . . Be sure you marry the right one."

Considering her own marriage, this sounded more like a dire warning than motherly advice.

11

Trials

●

n April of 2005, I moved back to the city I had betrayed. Ashamed of my past transgressions, I was petrified to show my face in a town that had once embraced me as its future. I was still tainted by the embarrassment I had caused the Bulls franchise and had no clue how I would ever answer questions from hostile fans about my idiotic actions, especially still being in such a fragile state. But I wasn't left with much of a choice if I was ever going to play professional basketball again.

Eventually I would work out with some great trainers, such as John Lucas and Joe Abunnasar. But *the* trainer was Tim Grover, who was considered the best in the game because of his intimate work with Michael Jordan throughout his career. Tim's résumé was impeccable—he'd worked with countless NBA superstars, from Charles Barkley to Hakeem Olajuwon to Scottie Pippen, and rising stars like Dwayne Wade, who was just finishing his second year in the league.

Tim and Michael Jordan owned a training center together called Hoops the Gym, a legendary facility that was known for training the best athletes in the world. Two years earlier, I was a 21-year-old kid who had arrogantly taken over M.J.'s former locker at the United Center, and now here I was in his workout complex with his trainer, trying to make a comeback as if I was some veteran looking to find one last hurrah. I was mourning my former 42-inch vertical as if I'd lost it decades ago. But I had to look at things with a glass-half-full attitude. After all I had gone through, it was a miracle I was even in a position to attempt a comeback.

Tim had once sustained a dangerous injury of his own, which made him even more invested in my quest. I have never met anyone more passionate about their craft than Tim. He brought a level of intensity, on a daily basis, that was infectious. We spent all of April and May strengthening my quads and hamstrings while adding bulk to my upper body.

Tim was inherently optimistic, but even he questioned whether I'd ever be able to recapture my explosiveness on the court. And if that was going to be the case, then adding strength would allow me to bulldoze my way through people. My hamstring had been torn off the bone, which meant I would have to rebuild as much muscle as possible through weight-based exercises—squats, leg presses, hamstring curls, single-leg squats. All of the original post-op physical therapy was still a part of my everyday routine

It was my own personal Groundhog Day. I had been doing this regimen six days a week for the past 136 weeks . . . two times a day. And Tim's regimen was no less structured.

6:30 A.M.: Physical therapy—mobilization and manipulation

9:00 A.M.: Gym—lifting with Tim and on-court skill work

12:00 P.M.: Lunch—while icing or in cold tub

1:00 P.M.: Physical therapy—flexibility and core

3:00 P.M.: Conditioning—riding bike or treadmill work

4:00 P.M.: Gym—scrimmaging or on-court skill work

5:30 P.M.: Cooldown—icing or cold tub then stretching

There was an ebb and flow of passion for the work I was putting in, and whenever I was really questioning myself, Tim and
I would watch an NBA game, and that was all I needed to get
"back on the horse." I had nothing left in my life if I didn't have
the game. I felt backed into a corner with no option but to claw
my way out. I convinced myself that *everyone* doubted my ability
to make it back, which was exactly the kind of challenge I needed
in order to get there.

As much progress as we made together, I still had a notice-
able limp in my stride due to the drop foot. Cutting was difficult
because of the amount of force I had to impose on my knee and
ankle. I accepted the fact that if I were ever to play again, it would
be done in pain.

Mind over body . . . and Oxy.

Tim was also training some of the guys who were entering the
2004 NBA draft, such as Raymond Felton from UNC and Dee

Brown from Illinois. He also worked with Chris Duhon, who'd decided to stay all four years at Duke. Chris and I hadn't been nearly as close since the accident, and I was entirely to blame for that. He was yet another friend whom I pushed away during that time as I shut myself off from the world. I was so happy to see him begin his next chapter, but very conflicted about it once he ended up getting drafted by the Bulls. He played for nine years in the league and is now an assistant coach at Marshall University, under Mike D'Antoni's brother Dan. I'm so happy to say that today he and I are as close as ever.

One time, Tim put together a one-on-one, full-court session between me and Raymond. He and Sean May had led the Tar Heels to a national championship over Illinois just a month earlier. He was by far the most explosive guard of the group and would eventually be taken fifth overall, behind only Deron Williams and Chris Paul. We first met when I was still playing and he was just a youngster on his way to college. Still a teenager, Raymond was determined to be the best and willing to work for it. He'd come to Durham every now and again to pick my brain as we watched hours of tape, breaking down play after play. His motivation was a welcome reminder of when I was once in his shoes, which only helped to fuel my desire to return.

So our matchup would go to seven points, and checking the ball was not allowed, which meant getting your ass back on defense without any stoppages. It was a drill done primarily for conditioning.

Working on individual skill work with Tim had provided me with a false sense of confidence. I was able to stop and pivot much less abrasively than at game speed. Even when I picked up the tempo for Tim, I was only competing against myself. My body was still limited by the soreness in my left hip, knee, and ankle. I was overly attentive every time I placed my foot down, scared of spraining it due to my lack of stability. "Gingerly" would be the best term to describe my training up to that point.

The truth is that everyone had been taking it easy on me. People were afraid of breaking my confidence. So Kevin, who was now my agent, working under Bill Duffy, asked Raymond not to take one possession off, insisting he give it his all.

We closed the doors to the gym and the real test began.

With the first possession, I was positive Raymond could see the limp in my step. While I brought the ball down the floor, he couldn't stop staring at my foot, which was supported by knee and ankle braces. He could see my entire hip hike up with each step in order to keep my left foot from scraping the floor. I settled for a jump shot that missed badly. As I tried to backpedal on defense, Raymond, with the ball in his right hand, attacked my left hip relentlessly. I was a stop sign, and he was a car running it. It wasn't the leg that did me in. It was the damn drop foot.

7–0.

In the blink of an eye it was over. On the last bucket, I grabbed the ball as it fell through the net and punted it as hard as I could into the ceiling while yelling every curse word in existence.

I knew it was my first time competing, but for some reason I thought—I hoped—I was a lot further along. I had to accept the fact that I was nowhere close to where I needed to be in order to stand a chance.

So walk away now and not risk the letdown to come? No one would blame you. I mean, you've made it further than just about anybody else would have in your position. Or keep going, Williams. See where this takes you. Worse comes to worst, there's always ball overseas.

Sometime in May, things started to click. My left thigh had drastically increased in size, while my calf started to gain definition. Real progress was under way, and that incentivized me to train harder. The real proof came toward the end of the month when I started to beat these younger guys on the court.

Drop foot and all.

One time, I blew by Dee Brown for a layup during some drill and looked over to Tim, seeking his approval. Arms crossed, he leaned over to Kevin.

"I think it's time we give them a look."

Tim had organized a semi-closed-door workout on June 6 at his facility for general managers, scouts, and select media to observe Ray, Dee, and me. Tim wanted to be in total control so he could dictate the pace and specific drills. Essentially, the workout was staged, since I had already mastered the "choreography" well in advance. I remember overthinking things while shooting around beforehand as everyone was looking to find a seat.

Don't limp. Don't get tired. Don't show them if you get tired. Look confident. No weakness.

It was the Nike All-American camp all over again.

While Raymond, Dee, and I were stretching, Tim walked over and pulled me aside.

"You have nothing to worry about. This is the same thing we have done every day. Just do your thing, Jay. Kick ass."

His words immediately calmed my nerves and helped to get me out of my own head. I attacked each drill with a sense of urgency. I forgot about anyone being there and lost myself in the battle. And once that happened, my instincts kicked in. Like riding a bike—just not the R6! I felt like I'd rediscovered my true identity in that moment.

When it was over, Kevin and Tim were smiling with pride. Kevin brought it to my attention that he hadn't seen me shoot so well since my junior year in college. The next step would now be Kevin accepting private workout invites by NBA teams on my behalf.

I was in the gym earlier than usual the next day, thrilled and motivated from the day before. While I was lacing up my sneakers, my cell phone rang. It was Kevin.

"Tell me some good news, big boy!" I said, in great spirits.

Always playful, Kevin began in a somber tone.

"Uh . . ."—deep sigh—"umm . . . We got Miami and Houston with interest, beeyatch!"

I dropped my head and clenched my fist with excitement. I had two teams believing in me enough to take a real look, when I barely believed in myself only three weeks earlier. Was it all really starting to pay off?

Kevin went on to explain that the workouts wouldn't be until September, so I had another three months to prepare. More good news.

"I'm going to do this, Kev. I am starting to believe again!"

For those next three months, Tim and I took things to another level. Guys like Dwayne Wade, Quentin Richardson, Bobby Simmons, and Corey Maggette started to show up at our workouts. I was on my way, and it felt so damn good to be with the boys again. It was like old times sitting in the training room, getting iced up while talking about girls they were dating, things they were spending money on, trips they had taken, and all the other stuff I had missed during my years away from the game. For the first time, my bitterness about this life being taken away from me receded.

I hit a snag about a week before my workout with the Miami Heat. I was playing pickup with all the guys when I mistakenly stepped on a player's foot and rolled my *left* ankle pretty badly. At first it felt like I had torn something in my knee, but after X-rays and an MRI, we found out it was just a sprained ankle. Tim thought we needed to play it by ear to see how my body responded. Therapy and ice consumed my days leading up to the workout, but I felt decent enough to go.

In retrospect, I should have waited, but I was anxious that they'd pull the invite if it got out that I was nursing my left ankle. I simply felt that I had no other option but to play through the pain. I don't know if it was the travel, my nerves getting the better of me, or just pressing too hard, but everything about that day felt wrong.

The first drill, I tweaked the same ankle, and it was all downhill from there. I turned the ball over like I was a third grader playing against high school kids. My shot was completely off, and I couldn't get around anyone. There wasn't even a need for me to stick around afterwards to hear the bad news. Nick Arison, a former manager on our Duke team and currently the CEO of the Heat, tried to talk to me afterwards and give me words of encouragement, but predictably, my self-esteem took a serious nosedive.

Maybe I'm not ready.

If Miami was a stumbling block, Houston was a dead end.

To this day, I still cringe whenever I see or hear the number 17. That was the name of the Rockets workout that would prove to be the most difficult drill I have ever done in my life. Usually, I was able to gauge very well how my body responded during warm-ups. And I remember feeling really good that day. The swelling around my ankle had subsided and I took an Oxy before the workout.

I was ready to go.

After warming up, one of the assistant coaches started to break down the first drill of the day.

"Jay, this is how the 17 works. You're going to see 17 minutes on the clock. The objective of this drill is to get as many shots up as you can at game speed each minute. You're going to start in the left-hand corner of the court. These seven managers will constantly feed you the ball and grab the rebounds. I want you to focus on catching and shooting as many shots as you can. Also be aware that after each shot, you need to have your hands ready, because the manager's job is to get another ball in your hands as soon as possible." I was comfortable with that.

Doesn't sound too hard. Just catch and shoot. Okay!

He continued to explain the drill as he walked me over to the right-hand corner of the college three-point line.

"The first 14 minutes, you will spend one minute at each spot."

He walked me through the first seven spots, which were all located somewhere on the college three-point line. He then explained that once I made it to the corner opposite from where I'd started, I'd move back to the NBA three-point line and do the same thing at each of the previous seven spots until I made my way back around to where I'd started.

He said the fun would begin *after* those 14 minutes of continuous, stationary shooting.

"Now, here's where it gets interesting. For the last three minutes, you're going to do the 'windshield wiper.' "

This meant that after each NBA three-point attempt from the corner, I would have to turn and sprint up to the elbow behind the NBA three-point line and shoot, then immediately sprint back to the same corner and shoot again—continuously—for one minute. When the clock hit the two-minute mark, I would have to sprint from elbow to elbow, also outside the NBA three-point line, and shoot for another minute straight.

Done, right? Nope.

For the last minute of the drill, I would work the opposite corner from elbow to baseline, baseline to elbow, until the clock showed zeroes.

Once we got back to the starting position, I was already exhausted from hearing him explain the whole rundown. He looked at me and asked if I understood how the drill worked. I nodded and told him I was ready. Right before we were about to start, he chimed in one last time.

"Now, remember, we're looking to see how many shots you make at each position, how many shots you get up at each position, and how high you will elevate for each shot."

I stood in the corner, knees bent, with hands ready to catch the ball, taking one last exhale. The clock started, and one manager delivered a crisp pass right to my hands. I tried to jump through the roof with each shot at first position, to prove that I still had my old elevation.

Bucket. Bucket. Bucket. . . . I hit the first eight shots.

This ain't that bad. Let's go, Jay!

Usually when a player does shooting drills, he wants to hold his follow-through until the ball goes through the rim. But this was rapid-fire. Before my feet even hit the ground, the next ball was already flying toward me with crazy speed. I had no time to gather myself, but had to go up for another shot instantly. This went against every fundamental rule of shooting. By the time we got through the first spot and moved to the second, I was panting, already in a dead sweat.

When I reached the top of the key, halfway through the first of the drill's three stages, my legs were gone. The ball felt like a shot put.

They don't want to see how many shots I'm going to get up, or make. They want to see if they can break me.

I was not one to quit, and I wasn't going to start now just because something was getting the better of me, so I kept going. I saw one of them behind the basket with a pen and pad, marking down every make and miss.

Physical hell and psychological torture all in one.

By this point, I was clanking 60 percent of the shots I was taking. I remember completing the first seven minutes of this drill and, as I was backpedaling to the NBA three-point line for the next shot, thinking about tripping myself just to get a three- or four-second break.

Things turned from bad to worse.

The longer distance from behind the arc exposed just how spent I was, since I couldn't muster the strength to effortlessly shoot from back there. I didn't have either the arm or leg strength to compensate for the weakness of the other. My entire body ached badly at that moment. My shooting touch was extremely inconsistent: some air balls, some balls that clanked the side of the backboard, some balls that slipped out of my hands, and occasionally some balls that went in. It was just around the 14-minute mark when I began to feel the entire left side of my lower body shut down—just in time for the "fun" and "interesting" part: the windshield wiper.

Every time I landed after a jump shot from the left-hand corner of the NBA three-point line, I had to turn to face half-court by pivoting on my left foot and pushing off that same leg to sprint to the elbow, then turn into a jump shot, also from behind the arc. The proper way to turn into that kind of shot is by picking up your left foot as you step into it softly, then swiveling your body on that same foot after you've placed it down heel-to-toe, until you are faceup to the rim. I couldn't pick up my left foot.

Minor technicality.

At this point in the workout, with my body beaten down, it was traumatic to have to hike my hip up in order to lift my foot and get it back down to the floor, while twisting on my left knee to spot up for the shot. I started limping because of the overall effort that went into each movement. I remember stopping for a second at the first elbow position and reaching down to grab my left knee, which ballooned with inflammation, as if I had a horrific allergic reaction or something.

I was no longer paying attention to whether or not I was making or missing the shots. I was past the point of caring. All that was on my mind was making it out of the drill unscathed, hardly the ideal mind-set for an athlete trying to make a team. When I finished the last spot and the buzzer sounded, I fell to the floor and did my best snow-angel impersonation. I couldn't move and struggled to catch my breath. I must've been lying there for a good four or five minutes when that same assistant coach from before stood over me and said the absolute last possible thing I wanted to hear.

"Time for the next drill."

You have to be fucking kidding me.

I somehow found the strength to get back up and gathered myself as best I could, almost delusional and in desperate need of another minute to get my bearings.

This can't be real. Another drill? Please tell me I'm dreaming. Wait a minute, is that Keith Langford from Kansas dressed in a Houston Rockets workout jersey? Why is he here? And why is he here now? And who's the other guy he's with?

That was when the assistant coach said, "It's time to get going into our individual one-on-one drills."

Are they trying to break me? It's apparent, Jason, that they're trying to break you. Look what just happened. I wonder how many shots I made. It couldn't have been many. I wonder how many shots I air-balled. Probably a lot more than I made. There's no way I'm going to be able to stop Keith. Yeah, you're probably right on that one. How are we going to do this? Who's this other guy?

He looks quick. God damn, I didn't know Langford was that tall. He's legit 6'4". I can barely breathe right now. I hate the way Jeff Van Gundy is staring at me. He always looks so damn studious. Am I limping?

For all I know, I was speaking my thoughts aloud for Van Gundy and all to hear.

Let's just say that the rest of the workout consisted of Keith and his friend blowing by me on the court. I had nothing left to give. All I had was my sheer determination to not be made a fool, so I reverted to scratching, clawing, and holding—desperately trying to find any way possible to not look like a chump.

Too late.

I was broken.

MY 25TH BIRTHDAY came and went, and the thought of playing again was starting to run its course. After another three months of training with Tim, I headed to Houston to train with John Lucas. He was the first pick taken in the 1976 NBA draft by the Houston Rockets. The thing I always loved about "Luc" was that he knew no other way but through the wall—never around it. He was old school. He loved to push people to their limits.

John's playing career took a turn for the worse when his battle with drug use became public toward the end of his career. He still went to therapy every day for his addiction issue, even though he had quit decades ago. I never told John that I was addicted to pain-killers, but looking back, I wish I had. He was always a man on a mission, and his steadfast determination to stay on the right track definitely rubbed off. So much so that I quit taking Oxy altogether during that three-month stint with him. It was the first time in over two years that I'd gotten myself clean, and I owed it all to John.

On the court, he pushed me like no one else, but at the end of the day, there was nothing John could do with my drop foot. The constant pounding of my foot, slapping against the ground on each stride, began to take its toll on my left knee. I had to sit out on a ton of workouts because of the bone spurs and the arthritis that found its home in my leg after years of training. Houston was not to be.

Back in Los Angeles, Kevin and Bill suggested a last resort. They thought it could be helpful to meet with a training group called Athletes' Performance at the Home Depot Center (now StubHub Center), in Carson, California, which is the home sta-dium of the LA Galaxy. They came highly recommended as a global leader in integrated performance training, nutrition, and physical therapy.

Upon arrival, the first person I met was a man named Omi Iwasaki. He was the head trainer on staff and was absolutely bril-liant at coming up with new, creative ways of working out. He put me on a nutrition plan for the first time in my life. Each day we worked on strengthening my lower core and increasing the range of motion in my ankle. After the first two weeks, I felt a dramatic difference.

While waiting to do cardio in the main training room, I found myself smack-dab in the middle of the entire U.S. women's national soccer team. Abby Wambach and the rest of her squad were there training as well. Right out of the gate, I could tell Abby was the ringleader. As I struggled on the VersaClimber, there she was, walking up behind me.

"Cardio not looking too good there, huh, Williams?"

I was way too tired to laugh but I managed to smile at her. After I'd been stretching awhile, Omi started joking around with me in front of the team, calling me homeless. Just laying into me about how I was staying at a Motel 6 and that I needed to find an apartment. Without hesitation, Abby looked at me and offered me a vacant room in her apartment in Hermosa Beach. I didn't know who she was at the time, and frankly I didn't care. I just liked her. I accepted on the spot.

After two months of training, Omi called me to his office one day. Exhausted after my morning workout when I arrived, I just plopped down in the chair on the other side of his desk. Omi looked at me with a blank stare.

"Are you ready to come back to the NBA?"

I responded with just a hint of sarcasm.

No, Omi, I've been working with you all this time just to be a better guy.

Just then, he pulled out a sneaker from behind his desk. It was one of my old Adidas court shoes that had been completely modified. A big elastic strap that was pulled through a sleek buckle was fused to the outside of the leather toe box. At the end of the band, there were Velcro strips. He held the sneaker in his left hand while pulling the leather strap with his right, showing how strong and sturdy the band was.

"Try it on."

At the time, I always wore an ASO ankle brace on my left ankle, and I began to take it off.

"Keep it on. You are not going to believe this."

After putting the shoe on, he tied my laces extremely tight, explaining that I would need to do so to provide double protection for my ankle. After the shoe was tied, he pulled on both sides of the elastic band and wrapped it around the back of my ankle, connecting the two pieces with the strap. The toe portion of my shoe rose about six inches off the ground.

"Walk around," he said, with a big grin on his face.

I got up out of the chair and took my first step. For the first time in three years, I didn't have to hike my hip up. The toe box being raised allowed me to clear my gait. It was as if I'd never had drop foot. Omi went on to say that I wouldn't have any issue with pushing off my left foot to jump because the band was elastic and would allow for that kind of flexibility.

I quickly grabbed a ball and we headed to the court. I moved around like it was 2002. I didn't have to think about trying to pull my foot up with each and every step. I could just run with physical and mental freedom.

That day changed everything.

It was time to celebrate.

I will never forget going out to Hermosa Beach with Abby and her friends that same night. We were having a blast doing shots and drinking margaritas. Noelle and I were going through one of our many "off" periods again, so I was out and about, chatting away with everyone. Later in the night, I was hanging out at a bar with a girl I had met that evening. We must have been talking for at least an hour. I excused myself to go to the bathroom, thinking about how great our conversation had been going and how cute she was.

Who knows, maybe this could lead to something?

On my way back, I saw Abby sitting in my seat. I remember making my way through the dancing crowd on my tippy toes, trying to see what was going on, when I noticed Abby had her arm around the girl. At first I didn't put two and two together, and then, after a beat, I just looked at Abby and said, "Respect."

AFTER FIVE MONTHS of training with Omi, it was time to head back to Chicago to Tim Grover and find my new NBA team. I was faster, stronger, and could move ten times better than when I had last been with him, more than a year earlier. He was fascinated with how the modified sneaker could make that much of a difference but warned how the sight of that strap could be alarming to all the general managers. It didn't stop him and Kevin from putting together a whirlwind tour of NBA workouts for me.

I ended up visiting nine cities in a span of two weeks. We had workouts with the Nets, Raptors, Grizzlies, Suns, Lakers, 76ers, Bucks, Celtics, and Cavs. All I kept thinking was *Now is my time.*

During my first tryout, in Boston, I felt on top of my game with my passing and transitional play, but overall, they didn't think I looked "ready." In Memphis, I was told I was too slow and needed another year of work. Philadelphia's GM, Billy King, was a Duke alumnus and really liked me. I thought I had a real shot there, but it just didn't work out for one reason or another. By the time I got to Toronto—after back-to-back workouts—I wasn't myself at all. I was sluggish and drained. Between the travel and the anxiety about each upcoming workout, I had transitioned back into my insecure self.

That is, until my visit with the New Jersey Nets.

Maybe it was having the extra day to recharge, or being back in my home state, but everything felt right about that day. There wasn't any limping, I was turnover free, I exhibited great shot selection, and my court vision was excellent. I wasn't as fast as my former self, but my feel for the game seemed better than ever.

A month later, I signed a nonguaranteed contract with the New Jersey Nets; I'd be forced to fight for a spot during training camp. I will never forget walking onto the court in the spring of 2006 and seeing Cliff Robinson, Vince Carter, and the great Jason Kidd. Was I really this close to making it back? Millions of kids bust their ass trying to reach this level, and here I was on the cusp of doing it twice.

As thrilling as it was to be there, my insecurity reared its ugly head once more, and I couldn't help but wonder if my tryout with the Nets had been an act of kindness. Perhaps it was a way for the Jersey-based team to help out one of its own. All I knew was that I had to prove myself worthy of sharing the court with some of the best players in the game . . . and one rookie.

As excited and as grateful as I was for the opportunity, I'd be lying if I said I wasn't disappointed when the Nets drafted Marcus Williams out of UConn, *after* telling me they wanted me to work out with the team. Vinnie Viola, one of the minority owners, and I were flying back to New Jersey on his private plane during the NBA draft when the news broke.

"Dejected" is the only word to describe what I felt. It was worse than watching the Bulls draft Kirk Hinrich out of Kansas days after the accident, because at least now I had a real shot. It didn't seem to be in the cards that I would ever make an NBA team again. My mind started to race.

If you wanted me, and really believed in me, what's with the Plan B? Or was I Plan B all along and too naive to see it?

The latter was probably the right answer, but it was something I didn't want to accept. When a guy who hasn't played in three years signs a nonguaranteed deal with a team that is already carrying 15 guaranteed contacts, he has no legitimate reason to be offended. That's just business.

Still, at the time it was hard for me not to take it personally; part of me felt I deserved special consideration for how hard I had worked. I never wanted pity, but didn't they know what I had been through to get back here? Making matters even worse: Marcus and I had the same agent, Bill Duffy. Even if Duffy's relationship with Nets GM Rod Thorn had helped pave the way for me to make a potential NBA comeback, it just didn't feel right.

There was also my relationship with Vinnie.

Vinnie wasn't just part of the Nets ownership group. He was an encouraging voice cutting through all the noise around me, a spiritual adviser of sorts. He owned a publicly traded company and still somehow managed to find the time to bestow his energetic and upbeat attitude on me. He helped me step back from the tragedy of the accident and focus on the positives in ways I hadn't considered before. We met while I was working out in California, and he put me in contact with one of his personal trainers, Jessie Chionis, who was deeply involved in a different way of training altogether.

While I had become consumed with the apparatus on my left foot, Jessie focused more on the mental equipment I would need. It was a departure from the way I had been doing things since the accident.

It's hard to quiet your body and hone your mind when you're suffering physically and in constant pain. The type of pain from training was a good one, the kind of pain elite athletes welcome because it tells you that you're doing exactly what you need to do to set yourself apart from the competition. I had really missed that feeling. The type of pain I'd experienced since the accident, however, only reminded me of my limitations. What I had lost. This new adventure was about getting it back.

The workouts Jessie had me do were rooted in the martial arts. I'd sit in a squat-like position with my arms folded, hands clasped, elbows pointing in opposite directions, holding still for as long as I could. I'm not talking about a few moments and then a breather, but 40 to 50 minutes each session. The goal was to reacquaint my body with all of the stabilizing muscles it had forgotten how to use, while also teaching my mind to resist the urge to give in, to rest. I had rested these muscles long enough; it was time to reengage them. While I would hold this squat, Jessie would talk to me about finding the strength to push my body beyond what it thought it could do. I had never done anything like this before in all of my training as a player. Here I was, slowly conquering the atrophy that had taken my body and soul hostage, and I was doing so with an unfamiliar weapon: stillness.

Hold the position. Hold the position. Keep your hands together, maintain balance, hold the position.

The whole thing felt weird, but it was July, and I wanted to prove to the organization that I was committed. I was going to do whatever it took to make the team. I would sit in that squatting position for an entire day if it meant that I'd be guaranteed a roster spot.

As camp unfolded, I realized that while I wasn't the same player I'd once been, I had developed a whole new set of skills that gave me back some of the confidence I had lost along the way. I was a lot better in pick-and-roll situations than Marcus, thanks to adjustments necessitated by my limitations. Before the accident, if I was on the right side of the court and the ball screen came up the middle, I could blow by my defender on the sideline, taking off as soon as I saw the defender's eyes pick up the screener. That slight distraction, a split second—before the screen even materialized— was all the time I needed to explode by him. The new me could see his eyes dart away, but I couldn't react quickly enough; I had to work the defender more into the actual screen, and then look to pass to my teammate rolling to the basket or keep my dribble and make something happen for myself. I had to become a better passer, and I did. I also employed other "old man" tricks, like stepping on Marcus's foot when I drove, and going up for a shot and throwing my forearms into his extended hand for a foul to be called. It helped that Marcus was neither in great shape nor had a good understanding yet of the NBA game.

But my tricks on offense didn't do me much good when it came time to guard him. I wasn't known for my defense to begin with, but even with my new shoe, I wasn't quick enough to stay in front of him. It was humbling to have to change not only my offensive game, but the way I played defense, too. My legs often felt as if they weighed 8,000 pounds. My body was tired, and it showed.

It wasn't all doom and gloom for me during training camp, though. There were a couple of days when I felt like myself despite my limitations. I could accomplish a lot with my modified skill set. I just had to try to get people to see and accept my game for what it was now and not expect to see the player I used to be. I could no longer be instant offense. I was now a setup man who could reliably get a team in position to run its offense. Although I wasn't nearly as effective as Jason Kidd, for now, at least, I was certainly better than Marcus.

Nonetheless, Marcus had this swagger about him that I couldn't rattle. We both knew that no matter how bad he looked at times, he was going to be given every opportunity to show his stuff. He was their first-round draft pick and wasn't going anywhere anytime soon. So I started watching tape of an old teammate from the Bulls named Rick Brunson. He had bounced around the NBA a little, but he brought this scrappy fighter mentality every single day. He'd had to play that way because I was the lottery pick; I was going to get my chance. He didn't have that luxury. Still, I hated playing Brunson because he was one of the fiercest competitors I've encountered on the court.

Four years later, I'm Rick Brunson. While Marcus turned the ball over and shot poorly, everybody kept telling him not to worry, to take his time. I had to tell the media that I still believed in my ability, and I had to play like it wasn't just wishful thinking.

One of our first preseason games was against the Knicks, and Nate Robinson was on the court. If you ever want to know how *not* fast you are, play against Nate. The kid just destroyed me the entire night, as if I had done something personal to him or his family. The worst part was, he was so nice about killing me, I couldn't even get mad at him. He would blow right by me for a layup and then turn around and try to encourage me. "Come on, Jay. You can do it. Hang in there," he would say after embarrassing me on live television. I liked it a lot better when M.J. was toying with me.

After the game, I walked into the locker room, my confidence in a coma. Coach Lawrence Frank started to address the team, and I just nodded my head, not knowing if we had won or lost. I was in a daze; I felt like I was done. I didn't talk to the media. I didn't even shower. I just put my suit back on and drove away from the arena as fast as I could.

After that night, I had a few good moments—the night we played the Celtics I made a couple of shots down the stretch that were enough to get my old friend Stuart Scott to talk about me again on *SportsCenter*. For a second, it felt like maybe I was headed in the right direction. But for the most part, I was only playing the fourth quarters of games, a big warning sign in the preseason.

In what turned out to be my last game in an NBA uniform, the play-by-play sheet for the final six minutes told the story:

5:20 | J. Williams—Foul: Personal (2 PF)

3:18 | J. Williams—Foul: Offensive (3 PF)

3:18 | J. Williams—Turnover: Foul (2 TO)

2:40 | J. Williams—Jump Shot: Made (3 PTS)

1:48 | J. Williams—Jump Shot: Missed

1:22 | J. Williams—Jump Shot: Missed

After showering, I walked to the parking lot, got in my car, and cried. I just sat there and let all the humiliation and pain and frustration from my hard work set in. I wept for where I was at this point in my life. I wept for everything I had lost. And I wept from fear of what lay ahead. For more than three years, I had wondered if I would ever be able to play again. This was the first time I wondered if I even wanted to.

Something changed dramatically for me that night. I felt out of place. I felt like I no longer belonged on the court playing along-side the best. Today, when I look at my Nets jersey, I'm grateful to have had the chance to play again. But the jersey also represents the moment I realized that the person I became after the accident was going to have a very different relationship with the game than the athlete I left behind.

If I tell you I've made my peace with this, don't believe me. I will never be fully at peace, knowing that my fate wasn't for lack of talent, or an erosion of skill caused by age, but rather a direct result of one stupid decision that refused to release its hold on me.

October 22 was roster-cut day, and I knew exactly what was going to happen. I was changing at my locker when Tim Walsh, the athletic trainer on the team, came over and whispered, "Yo, Frank wants to see you." His look confirmed what I already knew.

I had never been cut before, and I knew that streak was about to end. When I walked into Frank's office, he was doing paper-work, his head down. I sat down silently in the chair opposite the desk. He started the conversation with small talk, trying to delay the inevitable. Finally, after a couple of minutes of me pretending I actually cared about what he was saying, he started to sing my praises. The buildup before the letdown.

"Jay, I commend you for working so hard after all you've been through. You have been so impressive over this training camp, and what you have accomplished is beyond great, but I just think you need to go somewhere and play for a while. You need to get the reps to get all the way back."

After that, the only voice I heard was the one in my head.

Maybe my agent should have sold me differently. I used to be like a pit bull, but I'm not the same person anymore. I've been too nervous and shaky before the games. Maybe if I stopped overthinking everything and just played, things would be different.

Excuses had become a common theme during these self-reflective moments, and now I had run out of them.

My dream of making my NBA comeback was coming to an end, and I had no idea what to do next.

12

Last Ride

●

I n this life, a person is motivated by either inspiration or despera-
tion, and the latter was what drove me to make my next move. I
prayed that playing in the preseason for the Nets would warrant
a call from another team that wasn't as deep at the point-guard
position. But no call came—at least not from the NBA.

After four days of being idle, giving my body and mind a
chance to relax, getting back in the gym was my only option. We
were starting to get some serious offers from teams in Italy and
Russia for significant amounts of money. I was desperate to play
and was willing to go anywhere to do it.

My friend Graham had been playing in a recreational league
on the Upper East Side in New York City and asked me if I
wanted to get a workout in. Being inactive for four days seemed
like an eternity, and I thought this would be a good way to get

back into it. Noelle joined me as I went to meet him at a gym on 75th and First for a game that started at 8 P.M.

Playing ball with Graham always lifted my spirits. He was just as competitive as I was, and we always played angry. We were on a tear in the first half, dominating everyone on the court. It felt great to be back in my element.

During the second half, I drove by my man on the baseline and went in for the easy layup. As I landed, my right foot came down directly on someone's foot. I immediately fell to the floor, screaming and writhing in pain. At first I thought I had just rolled my ankle, but when I looked at my foot, it was positioned at a 90-degree angle from my fibula.

"Not fucking again. I can't do this shit. I can't!" I screamed.

Graham and Noelle rushed to me on the court while everyone stood around staring in disbelief at the grotesque injury. The guy whose foot I had landed on was almost in tears and kept apologizing. The guys picked me up and took me outside to a taxi. We rushed to the nearest emergency room, which was New York–Presbyterian Hospital on 68th Street.

When we finally got there, I was immediately taken to the back and put in a private room. When the doctor and the nurses came in, it only took one look for them to realize that I had dislocated my ankle. The doctor explained that he would have to pop it back into place.

He grabbed right below the toes on my foot with his right hand while his left firmly held the back of my ankle, and he rotated my foot until I heard a very loud crack. I screamed as they quickly started to put my ankle into a splinted cast to keep it stable.

We didn't leave the hospital until six the next morning. They told me that I would have to see a specialist as soon as possible to follow up, and for me, the only option was to return to Duke and see my physician there.

Duke confirmed the diagnosis. I had dislocated my right ankle, and it would take four to six weeks in a walking boot to heal.

I was beside myself. I had come so far and was on the cusp of playing professional ball again. I didn't care whether it was in the NBA or overseas—playing was all that mattered. The thought of having to walk back into the Duke Sports Medicine Center and see the same faces all over again for yet another injury was incomprehensible.

Three weeks of physical therapy every day with Jason was required, and as I made my way into the same clinic I had just left two years earlier, this time with my healthy side broken, I could hardly face him.

I could only imagine what everyone was thinking as I sat down on the therapy table, my right ankle in a boot.

Jason, let it go, already. Enough! *Why do you keep putting yourself through this? Time to let it go.*

But I couldn't just let it go. I was obsessed with succeeding, and I was not going to give up. I was only 25 years old, too young to let this be the way my story ended. I never once thought about what I would do if I didn't play basketball, and I wasn't about to start now. Sitting on the therapy table that day, I made up my mind to continue the journey to make it back. I was relentless. This may have been a setback, but it paled in comparison with everything I had been through.

Now I was doing therapy on both of my legs. I did the regular maintenance and strengthening on my left side while Jason attended to my right. Stem treatment and ultrasound were required, along with a great amount of mobilization for those three weeks. The biggest issue would be the bone bruise caused by the dislocation. Jason told me that it could last up to three or four months, even after I was able to run again. Icing day and night was essential to my recovery, so I purchased a Game Ready machine, which was a cold compression wrap attached to a mechanical device that pushed ice water into the wrap encompassing my ankle.

Two and a half weeks later, I left Durham for Los Angeles to see Omi and Athletes' Performance. After another week of doing stem therapy, I was able to take off the boot and slowly work my way back onto the court. My right side had always been the part of my body I could count on. Now, not only did I have limited lift off my left side, but I could barely jump off my right.

After a long day of rehabbing and working out, I went back to my friends' place to crash. I was staying with two guys and a girl whom I had met through Scooter Braun a couple of years earlier. This was like my little family out in the L.A. area during my years of training. Mike and Mike—not the ESPN guys, but Michael McCurdy and Michael Vukmanovich—both played basketball with Scooter growing up. We would always spend time chatting about hoops, among other things. Their third roommate was taking the steps to become a woman. She and I always had in-depth conversations about our insecurities. We were a cool bunch, and they were always nice enough to let me sleep on their couch from time to time when I needed a place to stay.

That night I received a call from Noelle. When I picked up the phone, I heard the urgency in her voice right away. I heard it in her voice that our run was over.

"I can't marry you, Jason. I can't live like this, and I just want to be happy. I need you to come back to Jersey so we can talk."

She was serious this time, and I knew it. When we hung up, I was certain we were done. In an effort to ease my pain, I went to meet up with friends at a bar in West Hollywood. I downed four vodka martinis and seven shots of tequila in about an hour. I knew I shouldn't have gotten behind the wheel that night, but I did anyway. While driving on the 10 freeway, I rolled down the windows, hoping the crisp air would keep me focused. I turned the radio on, too, which was not a good move. "Purple Rain" was playing; Noelle had always been obsessed with Prince. As I was driving, all I could think about was her and all the bullshit we had gone through to be together. I started hitting the steering wheel as hard as I could while I was bawling. It was like a scene out of a bad movie, except the cop behind me now, flashing his lights in my rearview mirror, wasn't an actor.

You have to be kidding me! You have to be fucking kidding me! There's no way this is happening to me right now. No *way!*

I started to pull off to the left shoulder from the left lane, which is exactly the opposite of what a driver does on the freeway unless he's looking to get killed. After drifting left, I turned on my right blinker and hoped I could work my way through three lanes of traffic without giving away my state of inebriation. I made it and waited for the officer to approach.

"License and registration," the cop said. "Do you know how fast you were going?"

"Yes, officer, I was probably going around 50 miles per hour or so."

"Have you been drinking?"

"Well, I had a couple of beers, but I totally feel fine," I said, as if my saying "I'm fine" would take care of the situation. I could hear the cop requesting backup, and I was thinking, *Really? Backup?*

The first cop actually recognized me, which led me to believe my chances of getting out of this mess were pretty good. We were having a decent conversation waiting for his backup, but when the other cop arrived, he didn't give a damn who I was. And truthfully, at that point in my life, I didn't care who I was, either.

I barely knew *where* I was.

"Do you know how fast you were going, Mr. Williams?" the backup asked. Again I said, "Like 50 to 55 miles per hour."

"Do you mind if we put you through some tests?"

I'm not stupid. Even though I was tipsy at best, I was sober enough to know where this was going, so before I got out of the car, I started talking about my surgeries and my leg.

"Look, here's my scar," I said, shamelessly pimping my three-year nightmare. "It runs all the way from here all the way down to here, and I have drop foot. I don't have stability in my left ankle, so it's hard to balance. I can barely stand on one foot. Whatever test you put me through, I may not be able to pass, but it's not because I'm intoxicated; it's because I can barely balance."

Awful, I know. I had just spent the preseason running up and down an NBA court, and now I was selling myself as an invalid.

The funny thing is, they put me through some simple tests and I ended up passing. I remember thinking, *I'm okay.*

One of them—I forget who—went back to his car while the other stood by me.

When he made his way back, he said, "All right, Mr. Williams, how fast were you going?"

"Officer, I swear the max may have been 60 to 65 miles per hour."

"Mr. Williams, I'm going to need you to put your hands behind your back."

"Why? What do you mean? What happened?"

"You were going 35 miles per hour in the fast lane."

When you start by saying that you were going 50, bump it up to maybe 65 max, and then are told you were actually doing 35, you are out of options.

Apparently people were passing me, beeping at me, and I was swerving, all while crying to some chart topper from 1984.

After I declined to take a Breathalyzer, they proceeded to cuff me, put me in the back of one of their cars, and drive me 45 minutes to their station in Van Nuys for a blood test. I'm not sure what my blood-alcohol level came to, but I know that I slept the night off in jail.

I got out of a DUI by pleading to a "wet reckless" charge a couple of days later and jumped on a flight back to Jersey to see Noelle. We agreed to meet in a parking lot off Route 18, between our respective childhood homes. She was driving the Range Rover I had given her, and I could feel my heart pounding as I approached her car.

I climbed in the passenger seat, and we found a quiet place to talk.

"I can't do this, Jason," she said. "I can't marry you."

Suddenly I couldn't breathe. I hoped that maybe our phone conversation back in L.A. was just another of the many ups and downs we had grown so accustomed to over the years.

"Why not?"

We sat and talked about the love we had. We talked about our first kiss as 16-year-old kids in her parents' basement. But we also talked about the hateful words we'd said to each other. The cheating. My accident may have given us a chance to address those wounds, but they would never fully heal. Not for her, anyway, and in retrospect, not for me, either. I didn't really know what kind of man I wanted to be when I asked her to marry me. And while I didn't doubt the love we had, she was doing me a favor.

Cut loose by my dad.

Cut loose by the Nets.

Cut loose by Noelle.

MY ONLY REMAINING option was playing in the NBA Development League with the Austin Toros. The team's head coach was Hall of Famer Dennis Johnson, the former Sonics, Suns, and Celtics guard. The man Larry Bird called the greatest teammate he ever played with told me that he wasn't looking for a feel-good story. He was going to challenge me to reach the next level.

When I arrived on December 3, the ball was given to me from the start. My right ankle was still bothering me a little, but I felt good enough to be effective. It felt like time was running out, and if I was going to make a move, it had to be now. Dennis promised me that he would play me at least 35 minutes per night from the jump. This was going to be a major adjustment, considering that with the Bulls I didn't come close to that, averaging about 23 minutes.

When I arrived in Austin, I had to adapt on the fly—I had new teammates I barely knew, I didn't necessarily have a great understanding of the plays, and I was still coming off an injury. I also was quick to understand that all the players down here were just as hungry as I was. No one took a play off, and everyone was willing to do whatever it took to make it. I had a new level of respect for their pride and determination.

After about three practices, it was time for our first game, in Bismarck, North Dakota. It wasn't my lack of speed or even my atrocious shooting that was the problem. The biggest struggle was that I couldn't guess correctly where guys were going to move while trying to pass them the ball.

My stat line after playing 41 minutes of play in the loss was: *14 points (5-of-16), 9 assists, and 11 turnovers.*

My performance was abysmal, but I chalked it up to this being my first game playing 40-plus minutes in three years. And on top of not being in the best shape, my ankle was still sore.

In the D-League, things were on a whole different level than in the NBA. Our travel schedules weren't even second class, to say the least. We played one game in Sioux Falls, South Dakota, that required us to leave Austin on Thursday at 6:00 A.M. to fly to Chicago, arrive at ten, then catch a connecting flight to Minneapolis at eleven, arriving around 1:00 P.M., followed by a four-and-a-half-hour bus ride to Sioux Falls. We rested in South Dakota for a night, played on Friday at 7:00 P.M., and promptly boarded a bus after the game for the four-and-a-half-hour bus ride back to Minneapolis, getting in around three in the morning to wait for a 6:15 A.M. Saturday flight that reached Dallas at 11:30. Our final flight to Austin was delayed, so we didn't get back until 1:30 in the afternoon, with a 7:00 P.M. home game that night. I'm exhausted just thinking about it. The D-League travel grind was just part of the fight we all had on our hands to get back to the big time.

In the middle of my last game, I felt something snap in my left leg, as though someone had just shot me in the hamstring with a BB gun. The pain was absolutely excruciating, and I knew immediately that I had popped my hammy. Later that night, I once again found myself in a hospital.

And once again I had a coach at my bedside. Coach Johnson

wanted more than anything for me to prove people wrong. We had made such an intimate connection as a coach and player in such a short time. He was a fierce competitor; he played and coached with extreme passion, because he'd always had to out-work people his entire life to achieve his dream.

As he sat on the hospital bed with me, he spoke about how people aren't defined by what they have, but rather by how they use what they have for a greater good.

"No more crying and feeling sorry for yourself, Jason. This is when you attack more than ever. Let all of this pain you feel accumulate and use it as fuel to add to the already amazing fire you have within. You just have to continue to fight to achieve your dream. It wouldn't be worth earning if you didn't have to go through adversity. You have a chance to inspire people, and I refuse to let you quit."

We spoke about everything that evening. I divulged all of the hardships I had gone through in order to get to this point. We talked for hours, and he promised me that once I got healthy, he would bring me back to Austin and we would achieve my dream together. He stayed with me in the hospital until I was released at around two in the morning.

The official diagnosis was that I had a small partial tear in my hamstring and had also severely pulled my groin. I would have to sit out for a long stretch, so the Toros decided to waive me to make room for another guard. Dennis once again assured me that he still believed in me and would welcome me back when I'd healed.

Another mission failed.

It was midafternoon on a Friday two months later when I saw a missed call from a 512 area code. I thought it could be Coach Johnson, since he and I spoke on an almost daily basis. He would send me game tapes and give me pointers on things I could do when I came back. We also talked a lot about my injury, and I always kept him updated on my progress.

When I called back, to my surprise, I didn't hear the voice of my head coach but rather that of one of my teammates. The first words out of his mouth were:

"J-Will . . . are you sitting down?"

I already knew that meant something bad was coming. The next words out of his mouth were that Coach Johnson had just passed away after practice from a massive heart attack. My heart sank into my stomach. I became lightheaded and dizzy. We had just had a conversation the day before about manhood and not accepting failure. This couldn't be happening; D.J. was only 52 years old and had so much passion, not only for the game but for his family and for life in general. He was a fighter whose spirit transcended basketball. But the reality was that his family had lost a loved one, the game lost a great ambassador, and I lost a friend.

I also lost one of the last people who truly believed I could still play in the NBA. I walked over to my back porch and sat on the stairs, head between my legs, sobbing.

What the hell am I doing? What is this life really about?

All the pain I had endured from training for my comeback attempts, from people staring at me, from the countless surgeries, from all the physical therapy, from the friends I never saw again after my accident, from losing my fiancée, and from the estrangement with my dad—all that combined didn't feel close to the pain I felt from D.J.'s passing. My father had told me years before that the number 22 would be a significant number in my life. The loss of Dennis Johnson on February 22, 2007, made it the day I finally decided to stop playing the sport that had defined me.

It was no longer my safe haven but more like my prison. The past four years had been so exhausting; I was obsessed with fighting my way back, but in the process I never took a second to see what I was fighting for. Something clicked that day, and I suddenly knew that I needed to stop trying to get back to who I used to be and start focusing on the rest of my life. When D.J. told me to fight for my dream, I always thought he was talking about basketball. But I realized now that what he meant was to live a meaningful life. And I wanted to get started right away. I was on a quest to find out who I was, only this time I was going to do it without playing the game I loved.

13

The Game

•

What agent doesn't cheat in order to get clients? They all do in some way, but the real question is how you define the word "cheating." Giving a young player a duffel bag of money for the rights to his future services might be shady, but it's not cheating, especially if the player or his family is in dire need of the funds.

It's called a competitive advantage, and Fortune 500 companies do it all the time. If you were coming out of high school and were considered one of the top individuals in your field, people wouldn't think twice about companies bidding for your services. Moreover, they would tell you to get the most money possible.

Why is it different for any of these kids who are trying to play a sport on a level that fewer than .001 percent of the world gets a chance to participate in? Because a committee called the NCAA says it's not right? Nothing is better than an entity preaching one thing while using a collegiate player's image and likeness to turn a profit.

These are the conversations I had on a daily basis with a mentor of mine named Charlie Grantham. I had met Charlie through my accountant, Donald Brodeur, in my attempt to start writing a new chapter in my life. Charlie had been a principal negotiator for a series of NBA collective bargaining agreements starting in 1978. He then became the executive director of the National Basketball Players Association from 1988 to 1995 and understood the league in ways that few executives even did.

The business of basketball had fascinated me since I was in high school. While I enjoyed the attention that came from my AAU play, I wondered who, exactly, was benefiting from my play? And how did they benefit?

The reality is that there are agents who take care of AAU teams. And though Amateur Athletic Union teams are 501(c)3s—technically charitable organizations—the kind of philanthropy they're involved in is questionable, to say the least. The AAU teams with the really good players are the ones most likely to be taken care of by shoe and apparel companies and other sports merchandisers.

Sporting goods being provided in exchange for a team's "allegiance" to a certain brand is really only a cover. Players and coaches receive benefits that go way beyond shoes and warm-up suits. And if one kid is exceedingly good in high school and does end up making it to the NBA, the "charitable donations" that a company made to his AAU team or coach usually give them the inside track on signing him to an endorsement deal.

As a teenager, I played for two teams—the New Jersey All-Stars and Rising Stars, both of which were sponsored by Nike. We also wore Nike at Duke. Given my track record with the brand, I think it's fair to say that I surprised the executives in Beaverton, Oregon, when I signed with Adidas over Nike after turning pro. I hadn't worn Adidas much up to that point, but I'd never had any say in the matter before. Other people were making the decision about what I'd wear, and they were the ones profiting from it.

This tangled web of relationships became the topic of my thesis during my final year at Duke. My research found that a large percentage of the players drafted by the NBA were raised by single mothers. Psychologically, this increased the chances for AAU coaches to become de facto father figures to these players; those relationships may have enriched the players' lives, but it would be a mistake to think it didn't enrich the coaches financially and in turn help athletic apparel companies build a pipeline to the players. I was fortunate enough to have my mom and dad around, but if I hadn't, maybe my coach would have been a bigger influence and I would've signed with Nike out of loyalty to him, whether it was best for me or not.

I discussed a lot of these issues with Charlie, and I never got tired of the topic. He would assign me 45 pages of the Collective Bargaining Agreement or a couple of articles to read, and we'd talk about them the next day. He pointed out that the rookie salary scale guarantees that a first-round draft pick will receive at least 80 percent of the set amount for his slot; his agent and the team are negotiating only over the remaining 20 percent (and a possible 20 percent more). That's why marketing is where the real money is, which is why an agent negotiates for 20 percent of marketing revenue. I found it all fascinating.

Say you have a player projected to be a top-ten pick, but he decides to stay in college another year and takes out an insurance policy in case of major injury, thinking it will serve as ironclad protection. Charlie showed me how the insurance-policy payout pales in comparison with the guaranteed NBA money the player would have made by leaving college earlier, to say nothing of the endorsement income they're losing. That's what I did, and at the time, I thought it was the right move. Playing for a legendary coach and receiving a top education were priceless experiences.

Players receive scholarships, and with the cost of a college education these days, that's no small thing. They also get expert coaching, great living conditions, and excellent medical care. College athletes aren't traveling seven hours in a Greyhound bus, either; they have private charters to and from games. It's very difficult to put an exact value on what all of that is worth, but we do know the value of the television rights to the NCAA tournament for the years 2011 through 2024: It's a staggering $10.8 *billion*, which is what the NCAA got for the rights from CBS/Turner. When I played in the Final Four in Minneapolis in 2001, the attendance each day was about 46,000; in 2015, at Lucas Oil Stadium in Indianapolis, the attendance was 72,000 each day. And the average ticket price: $250.

When policy prohibits players from participating in the astronomical profits their school receives, the system is broken. I wasn't even allowed to take my own shoes—shoes that the university gave me—and sell them to somebody, because that would've been an NCAA violation. They're worn in, with my sweat, but they're not my shoes to do with as I please? Even worse, my school and the NCAA could sell a jersey with my likeness, but I wasn't permitted to see any of the revenue generated for the sale? It's not right.

There has to be some way of compensating players beyond the college experience. And I know that question gets the most attention, but I don't think it's even the biggest issue. I'm much more concerned about the kind of education athletes get in exchange for their performance on the court or on the field.

At some schools, athletic departments aren't focused on the kids getting a first-rate education, but rather on keeping them eligible to play. An athlete will get a lot of help if he needs it to keep his grades up, and often that includes putting him in fluff courses to improve his GPA. The workout-and-practice schedule doesn't leave a lot of time for homework and learning; some of us want to be actual students and take the process seriously, but a lot of others are in school only because that's the surest route to becoming a pro athlete. And what happens when the dream of turning pro doesn't pan out?

There ought to be a curriculum tailored to an athlete's needs—one with an emphasis on economics, on communications, on business. I often talk to kids at basketball camps, and I ask them, "Who in here wants to be an NBA draft pick?" Every kid in the gym raises his hand. But, realistically, the chance that any of them will be is minuscule at best. If college basketball represents less than 1 percent of kids who play, then the NBA is less than 10 percent of that 1 percent.

With those hands still in the air, I continue: "Who in here loves math?" And the majority of the hands go down. I then ask, "Who here wants to be a millionaire?" All the hands are up again.

"How do you not love math if you want to be a millionaire? Let's break it down so you see why math is important. What money do you get paid if you're the first pick in the draft?" I

single out the kid who looks like the most confident. "Um, uh
. . . two and a half million?"

The answer is irrelevant, because none of the kids there—or
anywhere else I visit—know the correct answer offhand. But I
want them to think about *preparation*, about getting themselves
ready for the life they want to have and the thing they want to
achieve the most. So they *should* know what a top pick makes, and
they should pay attention to the details.

"Okay, the first pick makes exactly $4.592 million in his rookie
year. The salary is set by the rookie scale in the Collective Bargaining Agreement." If the kids learn the meaning of those words—
"scale" and "collective bargaining"—they're already ahead of the
game. But I keep going.

"So say you're the first pick. What are you going to buy first?"
The kid's face lights up and he says, "Oh, man, I'm going to get
. . ." and I immediately cut him off. "Your mom and dad have
been there for you from day one. So you're obviously going to get
them a house. And how much money are you going to spend on
your mom's house?" "A million dollars!" he yells enthusiastically.
"Great! That's a good son! But remember, you don't live with
Mom anymore. So if you get your mom a million-dollar home,
how big a home are you going to get yourself?" So then the kid's
like "Oh, I'm gonna . . . I'll get myself a million-dollar house."

"Cool. You got yourself a million-dollar home. You got your
mom a million-dollar home. How are you going to get around?"

"I'm gonna get a Bentley!"

"Okay. Nice. You just spent $350,000 on a Bentley. How
about jewelry? How much are you going to spend on that?"

"A hundred thousand dollars."

"So between the Bentley and the jewelry and the two houses, you've spent two and a half million dollars already. And you haven't even gotten your first paycheck yet! And what about taxes? You're in the highest tax bracket."

"What's that mean?"

"That means the government is going to take about 40 percent of your paycheck, between federal and state taxes. *And* you're going to have to pay taxes in every city you visit in the league, and you're going to have to pay an accountant to take care of all that, and a manager to handle your business, and a marketing agent, and . . ."

They look at me like I'm speaking a foreign language—and it probably wouldn't be much different if I had this conversation with most college players. But soon they begin to understand that it might be a good idea to pay more attention in math class, to learn a little about business and economics, and to know something about the world outside their neighborhoods.

Whether it's a radical idea or a more modest proposal—like implementing escrow accounts for college athletes so they may receive a small percentage of what their school generates off their performance if they graduate within four years' time and maintain a certain GPA—something has to be done to make college sports work better for the kids who play them.

BECAUSE OF MY interest in the business behind basketball, working as an agent seemed like the next logical step. My own agent, Bill Duffy, discouraged me, but Charlie not only supported my decision but brought me into a start-up agency he was involved in called Ceruzzi Sports and Entertainment Group. I jumped at the chance to learn more about the business under his tutelage.

The front money for Ceruzzi Sports came from one guy, Lou Ceruzzi, a billionaire client of a successful ticket-brokering operation run by Dean Kapnick, who was Lou's partner on the new venture. Before the Internet made ticket buying easier, Dean was one of the go-to guys for people on Wall Street who wanted last-minute tickets to any event in the city.

Ceruzzi's main business was real estate in the New York area. We thought we could get players to look at the bigger picture of business by showing them that after they signed a $40 million deal, they could take a small percentage of that money and invest it in a shopping plaza or something that would give them recurring revenue for the next ten years. We had the opportunity to bring players into massive skyscraper deals in New York that weren't accessible to everybody. Plus, they'd have the advantage of working with the guy who ran the player's union for over seven years because Grantham would be negotiating their contract.

The problem for Ceruzzi Sports was that the business of ticket brokering was very different from that of a sports agency, where it takes time and integrity to build trusting relationships with athletes, their families, and even AAU coaches. You can't buy your client's loyalty, at least not easily and reliably. And in the case of agents, unlike with tickets, the customer can always go elsewhere.

Charlie and I knew this, but Lou and Dean appeared not to. They already had an established and profitable business relationship and listened to each other more than they listened to us. I could understand them ignoring my advice, since I was a kid trying to figure out what to do with his life, but how could they not listen to a man who had been neck-deep in this business since the 1970s?

Because of my admiration for Charlie, I thought Ceruzzi Sports still looked like a good bet, even though I could see things were far from perfect. I wasn't playing basketball anymore, and, while I had saved my money, I didn't have any steady income at this point. I needed, and wanted, the job.

Our offices were right next to Madison Square Garden, and everyone was on salary. The overhead was ridiculous, and there was intense pressure to produce revenue at the same rate for a return on investment. Dean's solution was to toss large sums of money around to try to build quickly, which only made us look desperate. We showered money on "runners," guys who served as the go-betweens with players and their AAU coaches. They would pocket our dough, only to turn around and tell us that they had already promised to deliver that player to someone else, someone they'd been working with for years. We never should've been giving money to runners in the first place, but we had little choice, since no one knew who we were. We lacked the clout to quietly buy an athlete's allegiance under the table ourselves.

If it all sounds a bit sleazy, that's because it was. Even when we found a trustworthy runner—and I use that adjective loosely—they weren't stupid. They'd come to us saying, "Hey, for this guy, if and when he comes on board—I know you guys get 4 percent; well, we want half of that, and we want 10 percent of the marketing." They outplayed us at our own game.

Having been through this process as an athlete, I already knew that the best approach to building an agency was not to line the pockets of runners, but to build real relationships with players and coaches. Unfortunately, the mandate at Ceruzzi to turn an immediate profit permeated the office. We never gave money to kids, and we never gave money to parents, but we did provide some AAU organizations with money—a lot of money, in one case.

By the time I met Kevin Love, who was a freshman at UCLA, Ceruzzi Sports had already "donated" more than $250,000 to his former AAU coach, Pat Barrett. I knew money had exchanged hands, but I didn't care as long as it meant establishing a relationship with Kevin. I believed in Charlie more than anything, and although our tactics were morally questionable, all of our competitors were doing the same thing.

Pat arranged our first meeting at Mr. Chow in Beverly Hills. When Kevin walked in the door, I could immediately tell that he was slightly uncomfortable with my presence. It didn't take long for us to break the ice, and soon enough the conversation flowed easily.

I explained to him that the reason I was so passionate about my new position was because of the terrible mistake that had cost me my career, and almost my life. I wanted to help him make better decisions than I had made at the age of 21. I didn't know everything there was to know about being an agent, but I wasn't the agent. I was learning the business under Charlie's tutelage.

We talked about the agency, his aspirations after college, what businesses he wanted to be involved in, what his parents were like, and, most important, where he was in the process of picking an agent. I explained to him that he didn't have to pay the full 4 percent standard commission, that he could negotiate it down since he was a lock to be a lottery pick.

He hadn't chosen an agent yet and was still in the process of doing his due diligence; however, when the meeting ended, he did say how much he appreciated our taking care of Pat. Everything seemed to be heading in the right direction.

Throughout Kevin's recruiting process, we had built something of a friendship. We would exchange texts here and there about games or just about how he was doing. I would visit him throughout the year, and every time, things seemed to be just like they were before.

I had no idea whether or not Kevin actually knew that we had given money to his AAU program. "Thanks for taking care of Pat" could have meant a lot of things. But it was clear to me that Kevin was not the naive kid he passed himself off as later. He seemed pretty savvy about the game, and even though no rules were broken, he seemed way more comfortable than other kids I had spoken to.

We later found out that Pat Barrett had been working with three other agencies, and he'd shopped either Kevin or another one of his top players to all of them. Barrett had leverage—at one point he had Tyson Chandler, Taj Gibson, Brandon Jennings, and Chase Budinger on his AAU teams. In 25 years, Barrett had more than 100 Division I players play for him. Any college basketball coach knew he was the person to contact about recruiting those players. The man was an industry, and we were gullible enough to think we could work with him. On the one hand he seemed to be signaling that he could deliver Love to us, and on the other he was bleeding us dry. By the time we finally cut Barrett off, we had sunk north of $300,000 into him.

Even before this situation came to light, I was having a rough time adjusting to the agenting business. I came into it thinking I could help these kids, since I had a different perspective, with everything I'd gone through. If I saw them heading down the wrong path, I could say, *Hey, you probably shouldn't be doing this,* and they'd listen because they knew my story. But there's a lot of competition for these kids, and at the same time, other agents were saying, "Why would you want to sign with an agency where the guy just threw his whole career away?" I was forced to confront that head-on and talk to family members about my accident, the mistake that I made, and how it truly shaped me to become a better person. But I didn't really believe that—not yet, anyway—and having to talk about it all the time left me in a very negative place. It wore me out. I was selling a story that deep down I knew wasn't true; I had worked so hard to get my body to recover from the accident, but I still hadn't completely dealt with it in my mind.

When Yahoo Sports broke the story about our involvement with Barrett, my reputation took a serious hit. People in college basketball with whom I had had close ties started distancing themselves from me. I was hearing from close friends that competing agencies were also saying things like "He's not really a part of the agency; he's just a side pony, a name." And I wasn't the only target. Other agencies were saying, "Why would you want Charlie Grantham representing you when he and David Stern are never on the same page?"

Talk about hypocrisy. It's because of Charlie that NBA players are making as much as they do, and agents didn't think twice about bashing him just to sign a client. That was just part of the game; people would say whatever was necessary to secure a client or keep a competitor from getting one.

Reputation is all anyone has to work with. I know people talked trash about me as a player, but to the best of my knowledge, my integrity had never been questioned until I ventured into the world of sports agenting. I would go out to talk to the parents of an athlete and be told, *I heard from this person who said you're dishonest.* To say it was devastating would be an understatement. Yes, I wanted to make money, but I also knew I could help kids. I was trying to find my way and wanted to do something good. I didn't fully understand the ramifications of switching from athlete to agent. I didn't understand how I could be a bad guy when other agencies were doing the same thing we were, and painting *us* as criminals.

Adding salt to the wound, Kevin Love threw me under the bus when confronted by reporters. In explaining why Ceruzzi never had a chance to sign him in the first place, he said, "If I was going with an agent, why would I ever go with a guy who, no offense, crashed a motorcycle into a tree? I'm not going to go with a guy that reckless."

I get it. Kevin was backed into a corner and had to find a way to defend himself. I'm sure I would've done the same thing, minus the low blow. But I was absolutely livid at what he said. That rage quickly morphed into depression. I was lost—again—without any direction, and my self-doubt led to more drinking and partying as a much-needed distraction. Phone calls and e-mails flooded my inbox with interview requests to discuss the once promising NBA player turned rogue agent. There was nowhere to run and not enough drugs and alcohol to numb the pain. I would continue to do what felt like the devil's work.

We tried to recruit Donte Green of Syracuse by helping a family member obtain a credit line, and we got hammered for it. Some other guy wanted to fight me because I sat with UMass's Gary Forbes out of the blue when he had been talking to him for years. It was cutthroat, and it became difficult to tell the good guys—if there were any—from the bad. It was a "use or be used" system.

This wasn't how I wanted to think about the sport that I loved. Suddenly my character was under intense scrutiny. I was all too aware of the strain this line of work was putting on my personal and professional relationships. Perhaps I needed to be more patient about this rebuilding process.

While working at Ceruzzi Sports, still in a fragile state of mind, I decided to move in with some of my friends, since I had been so isolated for so long. Four of us found an apartment at 13th Street and First Avenue, in New York's East Village. You had to walk through the building all the way to the back, make a left out the back door, and go down a flight of stairs to the basement, where we had a four-bedroom apartment. We called it the Dungeon. The place was tiny and the walls were thin, which allowed you to hear everything going on in the room next to yours. It was the polar opposite of everything I was used to, and exactly what I wanted at this point in my life.

All three of my friends were bartenders in the city, so it made sense that we spent a lot of time hanging out at the places where they worked. Alcohol was a constant in my life—something to help the painkillers suppress my anxiety. I had taken Oxy regularly throughout my comeback to deal with my aching body. Now I was no longer playing or training, but that didn't stop me from taking the same drug on a daily basis to suppress a different kind of pain: the pain of failure. It was no fun walking around New York City, being recognized by strangers wanting to talk to me about my accident. Being high and drunk shielded me from the reality of everyday living. People could've said whatever they wanted to me then—I was too out of it to care.

I told myself I wasn't an addict, because I'd seen addicts on the streets when I was growing up. I wasn't stumbling or shuffling around; I didn't have track marks on my arms; I was functioning pretty well, considering that I was beginning to have trouble remembering things and felt like I was in a haze all the time. It didn't matter that my drugs weren't being prescribed to me any longer, or that I was trying to extend my supply by cutting the pills in half, or that I was taking them with other painkillers I could manage to get ahold of, or that I was falling apart while hiding it from my friends and family.

But of course I wasn't an addict, and I definitely didn't have a problem.

The first Monday of every month, I'd go to a bar across the street from my place and have one Crown and Coke after another while waiting for my drug dealer to make an entrance. I referred to him as my doctor, since I was no longer able to get my prescription filled. He was maybe 20 or 21 years old at best, and always good for a bump or two of cocaine to sober me up after I'd been drinking into the wee hours of the morning, before heading off to work.

He would enter the bar carrying a book bag meant for a toddler, which I always thought was weird, but I was too out of it to say anything. One month it was He-Man, and the next it was Teenage Mutant Ninja Turtles. I never asked him about the dosage or even attempted to negotiate the cost. I always had cash and just needed the fix more than anything to get through the day.

After we'd have a drink and some small talk, his hand would always tap me on my left thigh under the table, handing me a plastic bag. I would take it and put it into my pocket while handing him $500 in cash from the same pocket. Then I would leave, head back to my apartment, and pop a couple of pills.

Most of the time, I would only take one or two in the course of the day so I could maintain my high while still being able to function. People moved so fast and were so consumed with their own lives that no one noticed I was high anyway.

But there were countless nights when, after popping three at a time, I would wake up in random places or find myself at clubs with people I didn't even know. Just strangers I had met on the street looking for a bar to keep the party going. One afternoon I woke up on a subway platform in the same clothes I had partied in the night before.

It all came crashing down on me one night after work.

As I made my way to the subway to head to the East Village, an older gentleman stopped me, put his hand on my shoulder, and said, "Man, you really fucked up your dream, huh?" He wasn't finished. "You let us all down, man. You were the one. You really hurt me." My first thought was: *I really hurt you?* I didn't know how to respond, so I shook my head, let him rant for another minute or so, and apologized. I walked away in disbelief.

I can't believe I just apologized to a perfect stranger for something I did to myself.

I replayed his words in my head the entire subway ride. As I was walking up the stairs to the street, I saw a younger kid pointing at me, trying to figure out who I was. The last thing I wanted at this point was more recognition. The kid finally put it together and started yelling my name out loud. "Jason Williams! Jay Williams! You're the guy that got in that bad wreck, right?" I turned around, not knowing what to say, as he filled in the blanks. "I could tell it was you by your limp. Are you ever going to be able to walk right again? You still look messed up." A part of me felt like I needed to give him a rundown of all my injuries and the rehab I'd undergone just to get to this point. Instead I just said, "Hey, man, I'm not in the best mood today. I'm sorry. Hope you have a good day." I kept moving along whatever street it was with my head down, absorbed in my own misery.

Instead of going home that night as I'd planned, I went to the same bar across the street from my apartment. I sat there alone. There was no TV. I didn't talk to anyone. It was just me and my drink—and the two OxyContin I had taken that morning. I kept staring into the mirror behind the bar, wondering, *Who is this? Who am I becoming?* I was a complete failure. I was the heaviest I'd ever been—220 pounds. I looked at my reflection, and there was no spark left in my eyes. They were glazed over, and it was like I didn't have a soul.

If this wasn't the end of the road, then I didn't want to be around to see what was next.

I'd never really dealt with my accident. I thought I had, but I didn't understand that this was something that was going to follow me forever. I'd tried to come back and play basketball, because returning to the league would have wiped out my mistake. *See? I didn't throw it all away. I'm back!* But I'd lost too much ground. I kept getting hurt—either body parts that were damaged in the accident or other injuries because I was overcompensating. And eventually I had to accept that and quit trying to make my way back. But people kept throwing it in my face. I thought, *I quit. I can't do anything. I can't win.* I was defeated mentally. In a drunken stupor, I managed to walk back to my apartment, bumping into walls and muttering to myself. I walked through the building and kicked open the door that led to the stairway down to my unit. My bad foot got caught on the lip of the doorway and I fell down the flight of stairs. I just lay there motionless in a heap, with a cut on my forehead and the rest of my body throbbing.

You deserve every ounce of this pain, Williams. Too bad you didn't snap your neck.

I finally got myself up and into the apartment. I grabbed a

bottle of Jack Daniel's, locked myself in my bedroom, and emptied my bottle of Oxy into my hand. Only three or four pills came out. There I was, standing in my subterranean bedroom, wobbling from side to side, staring at the pills in my left hand, swigging straight from the bottle of J.D. in my right.

I popped them into my mouth, took another long swig from the bottle to wash them down, and dropped to the floor, my back against the bed, staring at the door. I took another long swig and hoped this would be the end. My mom wasn't there to stop me. Nobody was.

Then I passed out.

To my disappointment, I woke up the next day. Still in the same place.

I'd failed again.

DURING THE MOST difficult of times, I was fortunate enough to have a friend in my life named Carl Liebert. He was the CEO of 24 Hour Fitness, and he hired me as a consultant to work on the grassroots programs. Watching him interact with his amazing wife, Amy, and seeing the incredible bond they had, combined with how he raised his three adorable little boys—Jake, Seth, and Samuel—reminded me of the things I wanted for my own life. I'd been so focused on what I had lost that I'd turned my back on the values and principles I needed to continue to grow as a man. What kind of person did I want to be? I found an example in Carl.

I needed to change my life if I wanted a chance to achieve anything worthwhile. The first thing I had to do was conquer my substance abuse. I figured that was something I could do by myself.

I didn't go into a rehab or detox recovery program; I stopped cold turkey, going through withdrawal over the course of a week and a half, with all the accompanying sweats, shakes, and delirium, falling into unconsciousness and waking up to discover it was a different day. Eventually I started to feel better, and my mind was clear enough to give some serious thought to what I wanted my future to look like.

I'd lost sight of the need to balance work and the loved ones in my life. I realized that working at Ceruzzi wasn't worth risking my reputation or my relationships, so I turned my attention to another ambition of mine: broadcasting.

A little over a year before the Kevin Love fallout, I'd met a guy named Reed Bergman, who ran his own sports broadcasting and marketing firm. He came into the office to discuss becoming the exclusive marketing arm for our agency. As I walked Reed to the door after meeting him and his group, he turned, grabbed me by the wrist, and said, "What are you doing here? You have the energy and charisma for TV and should be talking about college basketball."

After Reed's comment, I thought, *Am I ready for this now? Is TV my new direction?* Months later, while still working for Ceruzzi, I called Reed to tell him I wanted to give broadcasting another shot if he would have me.

14

Mended

•

Going into television wasn't a new idea. I had worked a number of college games for ESPN2 and ESPNU when I was first recovering from my injuries, and it wasn't a great experience for me, the network, or, probably, the viewers.

I didn't know anything about doing television. I'd been interviewed on camera, but I was never a great sound-bite guy; at Duke we learned to give the politically correct answer, because Coach K didn't want anything taking away from our focus on the team. So if someone asked me what I thought about the game we'd just played, I would say, "Well, we did everything we needed to do. We worked hard, we ran our plays correctly, and we executed defensively." And if they got into more specifics about an opponent who elbowed me or something like that: "Well, I'm not really worried about that; my game spoke for itself, our team played hard." Boring, right? That was the point. It always seemed to work for K, but never the viewer.

Now it was my job to be interesting, insightful, and knowledgeable about two teams I didn't know very well, if at all, and I had to do it while learning all the simple technical things that everybody else learned in Broadcasting 101: whether to look at the camera or at the person who's asking me a question; how to think and talk while a producer is giving me information in my ear about the next thing coming up; even just how to have a conversation with a studio host, a coach, my play-by-play partner. And I had to learn those things in front of a national audience, in real time, in the deep end of the pool.

Dan Steir, head of college basketball production at ESPN took me under his wing, not so much on the technical stuff as in learning to communicate on-air. "Less is more," he'd tell me. "I need you to *sssllowwww dowwwwwnn*." I'm a Jersey guy; we talk fast. Dan would look over my tapes and call me, and when I answered I'd say, *"Heyyyy, Daaannn, how are yooouuuu?"* And he'd respond with "I'm good, Jason. I just watched a tape of you, and I need you to *sssllowwww dowwwwwnn*. I need you to e-*nun*-cee-ate." And no matter how slow I thought I was talking, he wanted it slower. It got very frustrating for me, and I'm sure for him, too. He was teaching me—coaching me, really—but I just wasn't ready to learn what he wanted me to do.

The truth is that at the time, I didn't want to be doing television at all. It felt a little like giving up, packing it in. I was a player! I still thought I was going to make it back to the league, and that was what I wanted to focus on. It was weird to be commenting on seniors I may have played against when I was a junior and they were freshmen. I didn't want to watch younger guys play basketball; I wanted to be the one on the court, playing against the best in the world. This was not how I pictured my future.

The games I was assigned to weren't exactly in the biggest markets and under the brightest lights. I didn't know all the players or even the coaches at places like Tennessee State, or UC Irvine, Louisiana-Monroe. I was on commercial flights with several layovers, making my way through airports on crutches, wearing a boot and a brace on my bad leg, which I still couldn't straighten properly. By the time I made it from gate A1 to A13, I was sweating like I'd run a marathon, not looking forward to being trapped in a middle seat, knowing that being in the air was going to make my knee and ankle swell up because of poor circulation. And all of these assignments combined paid significantly less than I'd made *per game* in the league.

I was still having frequent pain from the nerve trying to regenerate itself. One night I was at a game working with Dave O'Brien, who was a terrific partner and couldn't have been more supportive of me, when I had an attack of nerve pain that felt like I was being stabbed up and down my leg with a butcher's knife. *Pop-pop-pop-pop-pop.* I literally took off my headset and started to cry in the middle of a play. Dave didn't notice it at first; he asked me a question about something on the court and I just wasn't there. He covered as best he could, and then at the next break he put his hand on me and asked, "Are you okay, man? Are you okay?" I looked at him teary-eyed and said, "I'm fine," but all the time I was thinking, *I'm a fucking mess.*

Games I worked and players I saw in that period are all kind of a blur, because I really didn't want to be doing what I was doing. And on top of it, I was taking so much OxyContin that I probably didn't know what I was seeing. It was too soon for me to be out in public and traveling around; people still recognized me, and they'd get this look filled with so much concern and sympathy, but to me it just felt like pity and I *hated* it. Even today, if I see that look from someone, I'm quick to say, "Yo, it's okay, don't worry, I'm here, I'm smiling at you, we're having a conversation. I'm alive. I have my leg, I can still run, life is good, I'm good." But back then I'd think, *Oh no, he's looking at me, and he feels bad for me.*

It was all so unfair to Dan Steir, who was such an advocate for me at the network; I'm sure I wasn't anybody's favorite there, and he deserved way better from me, and so did ESPN. There was never any question for me that TV was something I was doing to fill the time until I could get back on the court. That's all I was focused on. I backed out of one game they had me scheduled for because I had a workout for a team coming up and I needed to get ready for it. The broadcasting business is filled with young people who would kill to get a chance at what I was afforded, and I just wasn't capable of doing it well, because I didn't care enough at the time to put the work in.

When I started working with Reed Bergman, he put me together with CBS College Sports Network, where I was lucky enough to work with a great producer named Debra Gelman. One of my first times back on the air was on a studio show running in conjunction with Selection Sunday for the 2008 NCAAs. There was a panel of analysts—me, Sean Farnham, Steve Lappas—discussing the potential seeding and who should be in or out.

Sean had launched into this soliloquy about how Arizona State deserved to be in the tournament—they were 35th in the Coaches Poll, they'd won both games against Arizona and a few more against likely tournament teams—and as he was talking, I realized (1) I had no idea what I was going to say, and (2) I had no idea who belonged in the tournament and who didn't.

They were working their way down the panel, and when they got to me, I just repeated a few nuggets of what Sean had said, and mentioned that I agreed with him about ASU. I don't think I could've named one player on Arizona State, though I can tell you now that they had a pretty decent freshman guard named James Harden. It was like when you haven't done your assignment in school and you get called on, and you come up with some bullshit and get away with it; there's a feeling of relief, but at the same time I felt ashamed that I'd been so unprepared, that I'd put myself at risk of being embarrassed on national television. I knew I hadn't done well, and when they invited me to do more for them, I was sure it was because of my name value and not for any talent I brought to the table. I felt like a fraud.

Even so, I realized that being on air had gotten my heart pumping again and brought out the same kind of nervous excitement I felt whenever I was about to take the court. It was refreshing for me to feel anything at all, and when Reed gave me another shot I started to think that maybe I could enjoy doing television this time around. It could be something to throw myself into, rather than something to pass the time until I got my "real life" back.

I was much better prepared when I went to the 2008 Final Four in San Antonio, where I worked with Greg Anthony. We weren't in the usual sterile studio setting, which can feel more like a cold operating room than anything else. We were doing our broadcast outside, with hundreds of people surrounding us. The energy from the fans and the crowd was uplifting as we waited for the show to start. While sitting in my chair with my suit buttoned up and the lights on me, I thought, *Holy shit, it's game time! I'm about to play!*

That brief time with CBS College Sports got me back on my feet. But Reed knew that the place that could develop and utilize my abilities best was ESPN. If they'd have me back.

I don't know if I would've given me another chance if I were Dan Steir. But I knew I had to go up to Bristol, Connecticut, and sit down with him to explain everything I'd been going through years earlier when I behaved so unprofessionally. I remember telling him my story over dinner, and how working for CBS made me feel a sense of purpose that I hadn't felt in such a long time.

He heard me out. And he gave me another shot.

I had worked only on games in my first go-around with ESPN; this time I was doing a mix of games and studio work. Despite my recent experience with CBS, I found the studio gig to be especially difficult. I'm not good with confrontation, which is typical for an only child who grew up in a household with parents who fought. During arguments, my instinct is to shut down and internalize my anger. That doesn't make for great television. It didn't matter if the subject had nothing to do with me; if someone said the sky is red after I said it's blue, I felt like I was under attack. And sometimes I *was* under attack: Doug Gottlieb, for one, never hesitated to point out when I got a stat wrong or stumbled on a name, and that happened all too often.

Doug is always very well informed and takes great pride in his craft. He's probably one of the best broadcasters in the country when it comes to talking about basketball on the fly. But being as green as I was then, I couldn't help but take his comments to me personally.

We did a ton of halftime hits my first year in the studio. While there were 20 or so minutes before the game would start up again, my colleagues and I only had around four minutes of actual airtime after highlights and commercials were factored in.

The producer would ask us beforehand what points we'd like to discuss so the host could tee us up properly when the time came. And when it was your turn to talk, you were looking at 45 to 60 seconds before "laying out," which is TV-speak for shutting up and letting your host move on to the next analyst.

Doug was up first and started to deliver his point. After about a minute or so, the producer jumped in our ears and asked Doug to lay out. But he kept talking as if he hadn't heard the producer at all. After another 25 seconds or so, Doug was still holding forth while the producer started yelling at him to stop. Once he finally did, the host then started to tee me up for my question.

While he was doing so, the producer said to me, "Jay, you only got about 15 seconds here, so I need you to be really tight." Listening to the producer, I completely lost focus on the question the host was asking me. I stumbled over my words and looked like a complete fool on national television. This was an entirely new challenge for me—more of an intellectual jousting that I had to become better equipped for. But Gottlieb made me up my game each and every day, because I was forced to prepare like never before.

Another of my many blunders early on was when we discussed Xavier. I had always heard the name pronounced *X-zavier*, so without hesitation, I say *X-zavier* on the air. To my surprise, a couple of days later, ESPN received countless letters from fans tearing into me for the mispronunciation—"It's Zavier with a *Z*, dumbass"; "You're a moron"; "Do your homework"; "Go hit another tree." It was crazy to see how riled up people got over the smallest things. This was during the explosion of Twitter, which only made matters worse. Real-time feedback was provided for me constantly.

In the long run, getting called out on my mistakes made me a better broadcaster; in the short term, it made me even more self-conscious than I already was. Still, I was really committed to this new career path, and I was determined to improve.

And just as things were really starting to pick up, I received some scary news from my mom.

WHEN MY GRANDMOTHER, "Grarock," died, back in 1993, it was from polycystic kidney disease. The thought always loomed in my mom's head that one day she might get it, too. In April— the same month as my grandmother had been diagnosed, and at the same age, 57—my mother was very sick for a couple of days, and I forced her to go to the doctor. I was by her side when she received the diagnosis she'd feared for all these years, and the emotional gravity of the moment weighed heavily on us. I knew that she would never want me to do what she had done for 11 years, driving my grandma back and forth to dialysis. I firmly believe she would have chosen to die rather than go on dialysis.

We went to the only place we knew, which was all too familiar to us: Duke University Hospital. Duke's policy was that in order to be put on the list for a kidney transplant, your kidneys had to be on the verge of complete failure. My mother's sense of urgency left no room for us to sit around and wait. We began to use our resources to ask for help—and we didn't just ask, we begged. Through two amazing people, Martin Morse and Scott Harrison, we were able to find a contact at Johns Hopkins.

On September 22, 2008, my mother was fortunate enough to receive a kidney from her good friend Christine. Just as she and my father were there for me when I needed them, now it was my turn to be there for her—to encourage her in rehab, make sure she was eating and drinking the right things and taking her medication. Her complaining reminded me of my own when I was hospitalized, but thankfully we were able to laugh about which one of us was the bigger moaner. When she was finally fully recovered, I thought we should celebrate. All laughter aside, she could have died. Just a couple of years earlier, I could have died. And yet here we were, still full of life and learning how to love it again. That alone was a cause for celebration.

I decided to spoil my mom with a vacation. She didn't really travel that much, except for a few visits to Aruba, so I thought a trip to the Cayman Islands would be fun. It was beautiful there, and our hotel—the Ritz-Carlton—was so amazing that we didn't even leave the room the day we arrived. We just ordered room service and watched TV. She ate about a quarter of the cheeseburger she'd ordered, before passing out. She started snoring, and I just looked at her and smiled. If anyone deserved to pass out from a food coma after all these years, it was my mom.

The next night, she wanted to go out, so we went to a nice outdoor restaurant where we were seated maybe 20 steps from the bar. We were having a great meal and talking about life. She was always the best sounding board, even if I learned as I got older which sounds to bounce off her and which to keep to myself. As we were deep in conversation about all we'd been through as a family, she abruptly changed course and asked, "Do you want to do a shot?"

"MOM!"

She gave me one of those looks that said, *Your mother isn't a nun*, and we called the waiter over and ordered two shots of Patrón. After downing her shot, she held the glass up and said, "Ohhhh!" smacking her lips.

"Mom, are you okay?"

"Do you want to do another one?"

We ended up doing three apiece. "Let's go dance," she said, after hearing Caribbean music coming from the bar.

After dancing to a few songs, my knee began to ache, and I headed over to the bar to sit down. As I sipped my drink, it warmed my heart to watch my mom out there holding it down, dancing with anyone and everyone. Eventually, she made her way back to the bar, accompanied by a—there's no other word for it—goddess. "I met this girl on the dance floor," she said, "and I would like to introduce you to her. Selita, this is my son, Jason. Jason, this is the almighty Selita." I immediately popped up to greet her and offered my seat. Selita then trumped me and offered the seat to my mom. She already had a leg up in my mom's book. She was the most beautiful woman I'd ever seen. I never wanted to stop looking at her.

"C'mon, guys," my mom said. "Let's do a shot!"

After a couple more shots, we all ended up back on the dance floor. Making small talk, I asked Selita what her story was. She said she was there visiting family, and I hung on her every word. I finally got the nerve to ask her for her number, and instead she suggested that we meet again the next day at the hotel. I had zero objections.

Those next couple of days were a blast. The three of us would sit in a different cabana at the beach, drinking wine and listening to music. Selita had this way with my mom, which made everything so comfortable. I'd look for music on my iPad and catch them chatting away as if they'd known each other for years. Let's just say she was off to a much better start with my mom than a certain former fiancée of mine.

I remember Selita wanting to change the subject any time I pried about her life back in the States. I figured something was up, but it wasn't my place to push. Instead, for probably the first time ever, I started to open up about my own story. I showed her the scars on my legs, explaining how they all got there. Pretty intense this early on, but it was cathartic for me, to say the least.

Selita put her hands on my leg and looked at me with genuine sincerity.

"I am glad you are good. Are you good?"

She barely knew me, but she could easily tell I was still a work in progress. One day, she revealed she was just coming out of a bad breakup. Before I could dig any deeper, she grabbed my mom to dance on the sand as reggae played in the background.

On our last night, my mom and I joined Selita and some of her family for dinner at a restaurant on the island. One of the hostesses snapped a Polaroid of all of us. I pulled out my cell phone and took a picture of the photo and sent it to my boy Martin, telling him I had met the girl of my dreams. He texted back almost immediately, saying, "YO, that's a Victoria's Secret model." After I replied with something like "Good one," he sent me a few links to prove his case. He was right. And Selita wasn't just any Victoria's Secret model; she was *the* Victoria's Secret model. But at the time, I had absolutely no clue what she did.

One of the sites mentioned how a couple of her past relationships were with New York Giants Pro Bowler Osi Umenyiora and the singer Nick Cannon. I had my work cut out for me. And I thought to myself that if this was where it was going to end, then so be it. My mom was happy, I was happy, and finally we were moving forward, feeling good for a change.

Before we all left the island to head our separate ways, I asked Selita where she lived, telling her I'd love to see her again. I thought it was meant to be when she said Edgewater, New Jersey. I was renting a place just ten miles away in Jersey City.

We continued to see each other when we got home. But things were different. It was my first relationship with someone in the "industry." Publicists, nonstop appearances, car and driver everywhere. This wasn't my life anymore, and frankly, I hadn't missed it.

It didn't take long to uncover the other side of her personality, which was that she was used to being in charge. Selita was driven and determined. She got what she wanted when she wanted it, and if she didn't, then it wasn't a pretty sight.

Especially when alcohol was involved.

One night, she had a friend in town and asked me if my boy Martin would like to join us. Martin jumped at the chance, since he liked his odds, considering what Selita did for a living. So we all got together at a restaurant in the Meatpacking District. His date ended up being none other than the greatest female athlete of all time: Serena Williams.

After making the introductions, Selita sat by my side while Serena sat next to Martin. Let's just say a lot of tequila was consumed at the table before we made our next move.

After dinner, we were driven to a club called Avenue. When we arrived, we were all escorted in by security and made our way to the table. Selita's publicist and some other friends of hers met us there as the night was about to kick into high gear. While I was making sure everyone was situated, the host got my attention and signaled for my credit card and ID. I walked over to him and was greeted by our waitress, who just so happened to be a former longtime girlfriend of a good friend of mine. She put her arm around me and I gave her a big hug. She handed me the menu and we caught up for a few minutes.

We ordered five or six bottles for our group, I handed her my credit card and turned around to head back to our table. Just as I looked up, I saw Selita gathering her things. Dumbfounded, I made my way over to her, and before I could even get a word in, she started cursing me out. I'm still not sure what I did to offend her. Maybe she didn't like me leaving her side to chat with the waitress. All I know is this beautiful woman who had been so sweet when she took my breath away just weeks earlier ended up being the female version of Gary Payton.

When Selita was done with her tirade, she bolted for the door, and her whole crew followed in her wake. The last person to leave was Serena who apologized to us for the abrupt change in plans. This lioness on the tennis court was the sweetest, most demure person off of it. I just told Serena that it was "all good" and that it was great getting to meet her. Then I looked over at Martin, whose expression said it all. *Thanks, Jay, for fucking up what should've been a legendary night for me.* Within a matter of seconds, five bottles with sparklers were delivered to our table.

No women and four grand later, the night was officially a bust.

Selita became distant after that night, saying how she needed time. I wasn't exactly shocked to hear, almost three years later, that she got sued for allegedly breaking another model's nose in a club down in South Beach.

I was an immature and spiteful 27-year-old kid at this time. So about a month later, when Martin introduced me to a really pretty girl whom I knew Selita detested, I couldn't help but pursue the opportunity. As much as I wanted to get under Selita's skin by going out with her, the joke was on me. When I first started dating this girl, Selita would text and call me out of sheer jealousy. I definitely got a kick out of it in the beginning, but it didn't take long for me to realize that the benefits were going to be significantly outweighed by the costs. The only thing worse than being with someone who ran the scene was being with someone who desperately wanted to be part of that scene.

The relationship hit rock bottom when I invited the girl to the wedding of one of my closest friends, in North Carolina. A night or two before the ceremony, I was out with the groom when he pulled me aside.

"Yo, man, I don't know how to say this, and I know it may sound crazy, but . . . I slept with your girlfriend back in the day."

"Uh . . . come again?"

She denied it, which I thought was very odd. He was one of my best friends and an ex-teammate of mine and he had no reason to lie. I couldn't help but think about all the times I had been unfaithful and dishonest with Noelle.

Well, now you know how it feels, Williams.

MY SECOND STINT with ESPN was going much better than my first. I was improving in the studio, learning to get in and out with my points, talking more clearly and *sssllllowly.* I watched as many games as I could to try to familiarize myself with every relevant team among the 350 or so in Division I—a much bigger task than knowing the 30 in the NBA.

I found ways to practice the skills I'd need to advance in the TV world. The host of a show should be able to have a conversation with anybody about anything, right? So I'd set tasks for myself on a day when I was otherwise just hanging out with friends. I'd say to one of them, "Give me a topic." He'd say, "Dinosaurs." And I'd make it my mission to get into a conversation with a stranger—at a bar, in a shop, on the street—for five

minutes, drawing out everything that person knew about dinosaurs. They may have thought I was crazy, but if I wanted to be
a great interviewer, I had to learn how to engage someone who
might not be in the mood to reciprocate. Besides, in New York
City, everybody's used to people who are a little crazy.

I also became a lot better at having on-air arguments without
taking it personally. I still don't like confrontation, but I understand now that it's just part of the job description. Everybody's got
opinions, and it's not my job to be right all the time. It's my job
to be analytical, engaging, and entertaining.

It's funny how things change with the passage of time. Now
many of my old teammates are at the tail ends of their careers. Mike
Dunleavy has played 14 seasons in the league, and it's been 13 for
Booz—they're both going to be transitioning out of the game, and
here I am with a 12-year head start. My boys are now the veterans.

In 2012, I flew into Hartford to do a pilot with my colleague
Andy Katz at ESPN. We were doing a spin-off version of *First
Take* for college basketball. Over the years, Andy and I have
become great friends, and while I don't know as much about the
history of the game as Andy—I don't think anyone does—I can
usually keep up my end of the discussion. I was running late, so I
sprinted from my rental car to the ESPN building and then darted
into the makeup room. That was when I saw Charissa Thompson
being made up in another chair. I had caught her on TV before
and always thought she was beautiful, but in person she was absolutely stunning. To tell you the truth, I felt like I was in high
school again. My palms were sweaty and I was fidgety, barely able
to focus when someone spoke to me.

I tried to ease my anxiety by striking up a conversation with
the makeup artist like I usually did, but it wasn't natural, because

my mind was totally on Charissa. Who was paying zero attention to me. She wasn't being rude—she did say hi—but she was busy looking over her notes and talking to everyone else. Charissa was quick. Her intellect and sense of humor were off the charts. I was looking for ways to break the ice, but I kept coming up empty. As she was leaving the room, I noticed the soles of her shoes were red. I felt like it was my last chance before she was gone.

"I see you have your good shoes on, Thompson."

She turned around, smiled, and said, "You know what Deion Sanders says, right, Jay? 'If you look good, you feel good. And if you feel good, you play good.'" And she turned and walked out the door. I sat down in the makeup chair, hoping that I'd left a good impression and wondering how I could bump into her again without looking obvious.

They say ESPN is located in Bristol, but really Bristol is located at ESPN. The campus is like a small college expanding in size each year. It feels like a new building is erected there every other month. Then there's all the star power that makes it feel even bigger. You can walk into any room at any given time and run into two or three Hall of Famers just sitting there, chilling. There are also a lot of studios, so it's easy to get lost. Fortunately, the studio where I was meeting Andy was the same one where they shoot *First Take*, which I'd done a few times before, so I knew where I was going. When I finally got there, I saw Andy at the desk. And next to him was the host—Charissa.

We chitchatted as the crew set up the studio, and I hung on her every word. She told me she was from Seattle and was angry with Howard Schultz for selling the Sonics. She loved Ken Griffey Jr. and was a huge Jordan fan. The more she shared about herself, the more I wanted to know.

Reading the teleprompter, she introduced me as "one of the greatest college basketball players of all time," then stopped short and looked at me. "Really? Is that true?" she said in a way that only she could get away with on live television. She then turned to ask Andy a question, and in an attempt to show her that I, too, could be playful, I interjected: "Charissa, don't you think that since it's Black History Month, that I should get to go first?" She started laughing, and I remember thinking to myself that I might have a chance.

Because it was a taped pilot, we stopped and started a lot so the crew could readjust lighting and other stuff. During the breaks, Andy always jumped on his phone to do his college-basketball insider work. Charissa used the time to look over her notes for *Numbers Never Lie*, a program she had to host right after we wrapped. I used the time to look at her. I spent as much of my free time as possible trying to get to know her better. We laughed a lot, and conversation came easily. We just clicked.

After a couple of weeks of texting and calling, she mentioned that she was flying to Chicago for St. Patrick's Day to visit friends. I told her that my cousin Jared and I were planning on being in the city that same weekend to see a Bulls game—it wasn't true, but I figured I could talk Jared into coming along with me, particularly once he heard the reason. Still, I was playing it cool; I said if we could get together, great, but if not, it was all good. She was open to hanging out, and said she'd love to go to the game, too.

When I got to Chicago, Booz, then playing with the Bulls, called to let me know he had left a pair of courtside tickets for me. I then bought three more tickets a few rows back for Charissa and her friends. It wasn't until I was walking up to the United Center that I realized it was my first time back there since the accident.

I don't know why it hadn't occurred to me before then—maybe because I was so focused on Charissa that I wasn't thinking about anything else.

Fans didn't recognize me. I blended right in with everyone else, and it hurt. Not that it should have. After all, I only played there one year, the team lost a lot, then the accident happened that off-season and the team moved on. The night I got drafted, I had hoped to bring another championship to the franchise. Now I was a forgotten man from a forgotten team.

My cousin and I sat courtside for the first half, then Jared decided to switch seats with Charissa so we could have some time together. Although she and I had gone out to dinner before the game, we'd been around people the whole time. Jared went up to her seat and she appeared by my side just as the weight of the whole experience of being back, so close and yet so far from the Bulls court, began crashing on me. I didn't break down in tears or anything, but I was more messed up than I thought I would be.

As I was sitting there, staring out into space, she asked, "Where are you?"

I don't know if it was the genuine concern I saw in her eyes or my need to release my pent-up emotions, but I began to share with her what I was feeling. How sitting there played into all of my old insecurities, how odd it was that the last time I was in this building I was signing autographs and kissing babies, and now no one knew who I was, nor would they have cared anyway. I used to feel a certain amount of electricity when I walked through these doors; now it was just another place, and being there left me empty inside. My stint as a Bull was a lifetime ago.

I didn't go to the locker room after the game. There was no

need to. Everyone I had played with was long gone. I sent Booz
a text thanking him again for the tickets and we left. On Sunday,
Charissa and I got together for brunch, but I had to head back to
Bristol for work later that night. As we parted, she reached into
her purse and pulled out a set of keys. "When you go back, you
don't have to check into a hotel. Stay at my place."

Here was this gorgeous woman, someone who could make me
break a sweat with a simple smile, and she had just handed me the
keys to her place.

Who does that?

Charissa Thompson.

And that was the beginning of us.

In many ways, this was my first "adult" relationship. Charissa,
too, had been through a difficult time, having endured a very difficult divorce. We were helping each other move forward, and we
continue to do so today. Charissa came into my life just as I was
finally discovering who I wanted to be. The angry, easily frustrated, spiteful, impatient person I was in my early twenties had
given way to a thirty-something-year-old man finding his way in
broadcasting and in life.

The uncertainty I'd felt for so long about my future pros-
pects slowly gave way to a newfound confidence. I was starting
to worry less about what others thought, and I began trusting my
own instincts. I loved being on air and traveling for work—while
exhausting, it was also exhilarating. I no longer feared people ap-
proaching me about my accident with comments like "Oh, man,
you had it all," because the truth was that I was finally starting to
believe that I *did* have it all. Working in a field I was passionate
about; in love with an amazing woman who protected my ego

like no other while challenging me to be better each day; drug free; happy.

For the first time, I took steps to surround myself with people who not only had good intentions but also were honest with me. Someone once told me that people are like trees. Every tree has leaves, branches, and roots. Some people are leaves—hanging there for a minute, but a gust of wind can come along and they're gone. Some people are branches—holding firm for a while until something more powerful occurs and they snap and break away. Then, if you are extremely lucky, you meet a root. A root is a person who holds firm regardless of the elements. I now have roots in my life. And those roots have anchored me to a very special place that I call home, no matter where I live in the world.

In the weeks and months after my accident, I began to notice how some of the people I had always considered friends slowly distanced themselves. The visits became less frequent; the time between phone calls to check in seemed to grow longer. When I was going through particularly dark times, I felt abandoned by people I once trusted and valued. I had been too naive to realize that some of the people I'd considered confidants were interested in me only because of what I could potentially do for them—a tough pill to swallow. The accident helped me cut through the clutter and see who my true friends really were.

For me, *friends* are acquaintances; *teammates* are the people, both on and off the court, who always have your best interests at heart, who stand by you through whatever life is throwing your way. Before my accident, I had a lot of friends, but few teammates. Now, I am fortunate enough to know who my teammates are.

My eyes are wide open.

15

Forgiven

•

n 2011, right after my 30th birthday, I had a meeting with an acquaintance named John Termini, whom I often ran into in New York City. We got together at 7:30 A.M. at Dean & DeLuca in the New York Times Building to discuss some business. J.T. was involved in global brokerage at CB Richard Ellis, and I was very interested in commercial real estate and wanted to discuss potential deals down the road. J.T. looked dapper as usual, like he'd walked directly out of *GQ* fashion shoot. I admired how he always seemed to have it all figured out.

Toward the end of the meeting, he asked me if I knew a guy named Carl Lentz. He was a pastor. I said I didn't, but I remember thinking to myself, *That's weird. Does he think I need help?*

"I tell you, Jay," J.T. said. "You have to meet him. He is going to change your life, man."

Because of Termini's overwhelming passion, I couldn't get a

word in edgewise, and all I could think was *Bro, I am not into all that stuff. Please stop.* J.T. told me that Carl had played basketball at NC State while I played at Duke, and he suggested we all get together to hoop sometime.

"Sure," I said. "Why not? We hoop every Saturday morning at 8 A.M at Baruch College. Bring him and let's do it."

Every weekend for the past year, I had been playing with a group of guys that included my old friend Graham, and the games were always heated and competitive. Perfect for a pastor, right?

That Saturday morning, as I was stretching on the sidelines, getting ready for my Game 7 (which is what I called my weekly Saturday game), J.T. walked in the door. Right behind him was a guy dressed in black from head to toe, with sleeves of tattoos on both arms. I thought, *This can't be the pastor, can it?* As they approached, J.T. looked more like the pastor and Carl like the one searching for his soul.

Just as people stereotyped me while I was growing up, I had done the same to him. My first reaction was to put him in a box, as we all are prone to do.

"What's up, J-Will? I'm Carl. You ready to do this?"

"Damn right," I replied. Then I thought, *Oh, man, I just cursed at a pastor. Probably not the best way to start.*

We were on the same team, and we dominated that day. Carl was a good player and extremely competitive, which shocked me. Then it happened—the biggest curveball of all.

Throughout the game, the player guarding me said some things that I took very personally. So my reaction, like always, was to become lost in the battle. As I was running down the court without the basketball, my man decided to check me with his elbow right in my chest. My first reaction was to swing right back at him. But before I even had a chance, Carl—a man I had met less than an hour ago—put himself in harm's way to defend me. I was stunned. A pastor was on the verge of getting into a fight to protect a man he barely knew. Carl intrigued me enough that I decided to attend his sermon the next morning.

I had never been to Hillsong Church before, but something about the place felt special. Everyone was around my age, and the energy in the building was palpable. The music wasn't typical church music; it looked and sounded as if there were a rock band on stage. Drummers were playing beats that had me swaying from side to side like I was in a club. And the voices and lyrics had such an effect on me, they nearly brought me to tears.

It felt to me as though everyone in attendance had gone through something traumatic in their lives that had compelled them to be here. We were all looking for a community of people we could rely on to hold us up rather than knock us down. Hands were in the air, eyes were closed; these people believed in something bigger than themselves. This felt like a new team. This felt like a family.

As I started to give in and become vulnerable enough to let my arms and hands extend toward the ceiling, the music began to slow down and the lights dimmed. I heard the same voice from the day before on the court.

Carl's ability to dance verbally with the crowd and keep every single listener engaged in the conversation was extraordinary. His words were so dynamic that they kept me on the edge of my seat. His sermon that day was called "That Girl Is Poison." Yes, the song by Bell Biv DeVoe. Carl used it as a metaphor for how one wrong move can poison your potential and how it usually happens when you least expect it.

Although the song was about a bunch of guys trying to tell a friend that his girl was bad news, Carl talked about how there are all kinds of poison in life. "That *mentality* is poison," he said. "That *attitude* is poison. That *seed* that someone planted that still affects the way you see yourself is poison."

I stood there, staring at Carl in awe. I felt like he was speaking directly to me. My life up until that point had been filled with poison. The Oxy, the alcohol, the people trying to tear me down, my insecurity, my anger, my spitefulness—all poison.

He said, "I am so tired of people circling around the same mountain, falling into the same traps." I couldn't help but reflect on the years I had spent feeling lost and sorry for myself. I was disgusted with myself for twice wanting to throw away this special gift of life.

I clung to every word Carl uttered that day. The man truly moved me. His words were pushing me to places I had never been before, and after the sermon was over, he looked directly at me as he asked the congregation, "Are you ready for a change in your life?"

And Carl Lentz has been by my side ever since.

He and the church helped me realize that part of being a better, stronger man meant giving to others what I hoped to receive in return: understanding, acceptance, love, and encouragement. It was okay to be vulnerable—emotionally, spiritually, open to real change. But no one has all the answers. In the early stages of my rehabilitation, I was so focused on the things I couldn't do that I often forgot to give myself credit for the milestones I reached. If I wasn't going to acknowledge my own personal growth, how could I possibly appreciate the sacrifices other people had made for me?

My relationship with my dad had always been complicated. When I was growing up, he was often absent, either working long hours or traveling for business. And when he was home, he brought his tension and stress with him. And every now and again, for both of them, it boiled over into something dark.

As difficult as it has been for my mom and me to get past what we endured, I think it's been even more of a struggle for my dad to come to terms with it. For as long as I can remember, he emphasized the importance of taking responsibility for one's actions. When I was four or five years old, I was in the yard playing baseball with my dad when I hit a ball that broke our neighbor's window. The Rengas were like family, but I was still terrified of their reaction. I wanted to run up to my room and hide, but my dad told me that real men accept the consequences of their actions, so we walked next door together. When Mr. Renga, the patriarch, came to the door, I glanced at my dad as he held my hand, then confessed and apologized for what I had done.

My dad had to scrape and fight for everything in his life, and he wanted me to know what it was like to have to work for the things I wanted. He taught me that life is full of obstacles, and it would always be up to me to figure out a way to overcome them. In the aftermath of the accident, I relied on those early lessons to get me through my recovery. To walk again. To run again. To dare to play again. And, most painful of all, to find the strength to build a life when playing ball could no longer be a part of it.

My dad took pride in teaching me the difference between right and wrong, and having to admit that he was the source of so much pain for his family has been no easy task. I know that the man he is today would never lay a hand on anyone. My parents remain legally married and speak daily, but they continue to live separately and have done so for years. And while my mother doesn't like to dwell on the past, I know she certainly hasn't forgotten it, either. But there are things about my dad that my mom will always value. It would be impossible not to. When I was in the hospital, he was her rock, offering her comfort and reassurance when the doctors weren't sure if I would ever walk again.

In order to have a relationship with him, I had to let go of the animosity and the bitterness. He had taught me how to be a good person, even if he was still figuring out how to be one himself.

I love my father and I accept him for who he was then and who he is now. Of course, his health struggles have brought us even closer. Several years ago, he had a series of epileptic seizures. They have caused neurological disruptions that affect his short-term memory; for a man who values order and control as much as he does, the unpredictability of the seizures has been unbearable for him. Seeing him this way has made it easier for me to empathize with him, and, as his son, I feel a responsibility to take care of him the same way he took care of me when I needed him the most. It was time to forgive my dad and move forward.

What was next would be the most challenging of all: forgiving myself.

For much of my life, I carried an immeasurable amount of guilt that I couldn't protect my mom when I was a child. That guilt was further complicated by my accident. When I signed with the Bulls, I promised myself that I would see to it that my family and friends, especially my mom, were taken care of financially. I was determined to give them a new life. My parents had worked so hard all their lives, and all I wanted to do was reward them. When it became clear that I would never play ball again, I blamed myself for putting my family's stability at risk.

Knowing that the only person I had to blame for the accident was myself left me angry. Lying in the hospital bed, I thought of all the people I had let down. I was mad at myself for not listening to voices of reason. I was mad at myself for not letting go of the bike when I felt it slip into gear. Mostly, I was furious with myself for throwing away a dream I had spent so many years trying to reach.

The psychological battle was the most arduous one, because it never stopped. Even close to ten years after I was discharged from the hospital, I would sit alone in my room and think about how unworthy I was of the love and care my inner circle gave me. I had cheated on Noelle, and yet she came to North Carolina and cared for me without hesitation. My mom had dropped everything and jeopardized her marriage, all for my benefit. My dad had been robbed of his dream to run a family business. I couldn't take it anymore. For a time, the only way I could shut out the pain and anger was by self-medicating. I hated myself, and eventually I reached a point where I didn't think life was worth living. I was consumed by depression and bitterness and felt like the only option was to take my own life.

My psychotherapist encouraged me to embrace every emotion—sadness, fear, anger—as they bubbled up to the surface. Until I could acknowledge the validity of each reaction, I wouldn't be able to truly face down my demons. We all make mistakes, apologize to those we've wronged, ask for forgiveness. There's a lot of power in that approach; forgiveness not only frees the perpetrator, but the victim as well. In my case, I was both transgressor and victim. For so long, holding on to pain and disappointment had been as natural as breathing.

Many people make bad decisions and walk away unscathed. Some of us aren't as fortunate, forced to pay the price for a life-altering mistake. But if we're lucky, we're able to eventually learn from our mistakes and move on with our lives. To this day I am judged regularly for an accident that occurred a lifetime ago, but I know that I have a choice every day to either feel sorry for myself and continue to let the accident define me or to forgive myself and appreciate the second chance I have been given.

I choose the latter.

I understand that it's an important part of my story, but it's a turning point, not an ending. I won't let it be my whole story.

When I first played at Duke, the game was so much faster than I'd ever realized. It seemed like it was being played at 8,000 miles per hour. By my sophomore year, as I found my way, things slowed down. I had more clarity, and I made decisions with ease. I didn't force the action but instead let the play reveal itself.

Finally, more than ten years later, the same holds true for my life off the court. When you move at warp speed, you don't really take the time to think about all of the small things that have accumulated to make your life what it is. There's a tendency not to reflect on the past, because you're so caught up in the frustration and anger of the present.

My life has always had a purpose. I had just been too obsessed with trying to recover what I'd lost instead of focusing on what I'd found. That's when I realized there are no accidents in this life. The choices I made were ones that reflected who I was at that time—a decision made by a 21-year-old kid whom my 34-year-old self would barely recognize.

I've been asked many times what I would say to my younger

self. I never answered the question, because I honestly didn't know. Of course, it's easy to say I should have grabbed the keys to the Corvette, but would I truly be the man I am today had it not been for the journey?

Up until that fateful day, I needed recognition and affirmation from everyone. I was so insecure that I needed to fight the ones I loved the most in order to feel in control. I was just a scared kid pretending to have it all figured out. The truth is that, at 21 years young, nobody really has anything figured out. You have to live life and experience things to gain perspective. And you make mistakes along the way, while hopefully learning from them in order to grow.

Because of all that I have been through, I never lose faith regardless of any challenge that lingers just around the corner. I've discovered how to love, how to truly work for something I want, and how to accept others and look past their faults. I know where I am and I know how I got here; this was my path, and my hope for others is that they accept theirs as well.

The fact is that I have been "playing small" for a very long time by not telling my story. I have spent too much time afraid of opening myself up to the outside world and sharing my inner thoughts because of people's inclination to judge. It's easy to draw conclusions about my family, my love life, my job, and the choices I've made. It's up to me whether I choose to let those outside voices dictate how I live my life.

It's time to stop pushing the pain away and to start accepting and embracing it. I accept the decision I made that ruined my future in professional basketball. I embrace that decision because I know that my road forward requires a road traveled.

I spent so much of my life following a specific set of plans,

from graduating college to playing in the NBA to enduring physical therapy to getting back in the league. I'm done conforming
to a blueprint.

Sure, I have plans for the future, but I know things aren't
always going to work out the way I intend them to, and I'll be
ready for it this time.

Acknowledgments

●

First and foremost, giving thanks to my source is my priority. Without my faith in God, I would've never been strong enough to battle through all the years of pain and share my story with you today.

When I first decided to try to write this book three years ago, a lot of people turned me down, stating that it made no sense for me to write a memoir at the age of 31. They all said, "You should wait until you are a lot older," to which I adamantly disagreed. If there was anything my journey had taught me, it was that nothing in this life is guaranteed. Every day is a gift and a blessing. Thank you to HarperCollins and David Hirshey for believing in me on this project and having the patience to stick with me through this three-year process.

Everyone in this life has experienced some kind of emotional pain. We all have had an "accident" in some form or fashion.

Whether that be a motorcycle crash, the loss of a loved one, a divorce, family issues, losing your job, physical abuse, emotional abuse, and so on. It's how you deal with that adversity that will determine who you will become.

> God grant me the serenity to accept
> the things I cannot change, the courage
> to change the things I can and the wisdom
> to know the difference.

I have made a lot of mistakes in my life, and I owe a huge thank-you to the people who have forced me to confront my wrongs. Thank you to Coach K, who taught me how to be a fighter and live my life with principle each and every day. You still serve as a moral compass in my life, and for that I will be forever grateful. Thank you to Charles Grantham, who still inspires me each day to be smarter and better myself intellectually. Much gratitude to Noelle, whose journey was a tumultuous experience, but we still remain friends to this day. Thank you to Carl Liebert, who served a significant role in my life during my time of being lost and in pain. You, Amy, Seth, Jacob, and Samuel mean the world to me. A momentous thank you to my agent, Evan Dick, who pushed me to make this book exactly what it should have been in the first place. Your relentless ambition and commitment to our work has bonded us as brothers for life my friend. Thank you to RR and JN, for all of their thoughtful help in the process of selection and editing. Thanks to Charissa, who has read over the book multiple times and has always been patient with me as I exposed my true self to her step-by-step. And most important, to my mother and my father, who have always been the light in my life and continue to be. Each day they fought for me and sacrificed in order to help me achieve my dreams. Thank you for believing in me when no one else did, and always keeping me focused on the prize that is living this life openly and honestly while being happy.

And last but not least, I beg forgiveness to all of those who have been with me over the course of the years and whose names I have failed to mention. I owe the biggest gratitude to those relationships, both good and bad, because they have all led me to become the person I am today.

I leave you with this:

The past should be left in the past or it can steal your future. Live life for what today can bring and not what yesterday has taken away.

About the Author

●

Jay Williams is a former professional basketball player and current ESPN analyst. While at Duke, he won the Naismith College Player of the Year Award, was named the AP Player of the Year in 2002, and was a unanimous first-team All-American. He was drafted by the Chicago Bulls as the second overall pick in the 2002 NBA draft. He is a motivational speaker, president of the JW Group, managing partner of the Leverage Agency, and a committed member of a number of charities.